THE BASICS OF ECOLOGY

CORE CONCEPTS

THE BASICS OF ECOLOGY

ANNE O'DALY

ROSEN PUBLISHING
NEW YORK

Published in 2023 by The Rosen Publishing Group, Inc.
29 East 21st Street, New York, NY 10010

Text and Editor: Lindsey Lowe
Children's Publisher: Anne O'Daly
Design Manager: Keith Davis
Picture Manager: Sophie Mortimer

Cataloging-in-Publication Data

Names: O'Daly, Anne.
Title: The basics of ecology / Anne O'Daly.
Description: Second edition. | New York : Rosen YA, 2023. | Series: Core concepts | Includes glossary and index.
Identifiers: ISBN 9781499473414 (pbk.) | ISBN 9781499473421 (library bound) | ISBN 9781499473438 (ebook)
Subjects: LCSH: Ecology--Juvenile literature. | Habitat (Ecology)--Juvenile literature.
Classification: LCC QH541.14 O339 2023 | DDC 577--dc23

Manufactured in the United States of America

CPSIA Compliance Information: Batch #CSRYA23. For further information, contact Rosen Publishing, New York, New York, at 1-800-237-9932.

CONTENTS

CHAPTER 1

What Is Ecology?

Ecology is the branch of science that studies living things, their environment, and their relationships with each other.

Every living organism depends on other things for its survival. House sparrows in a park have to find seeds to eat. The seeds come from plants that need a place to grow. Sparrows feed on insects, too, and the insects need plants to eat. Sparrows also need air to breathe, water to drink, and places to lay eggs. Each sparrow is at the center of a network involving other living things and their surroundings, or environment. Ecology is the science that studies these types of relationships. Instead of concentrating only on a sparrow, ecologists study its interaction with other organisms and its environment.

A gypsy moth caterpillar. Many caterpillars eat leaves, and many birds then eat the caterpillars. This link between leaf, caterpillar, and bird forms a food chain.

What Are Food Chains and Webs?

One of the most basic ideas in ecology is the food chain. Green plants make food from water, sunlight, and carbon dioxide (in the air) through a process called photosynthesis. Animals cannot do this, so they must eat other living organisms to get their food.

Caterpillars eat leaves. In a simple food chain other animals, such as small birds, eat the caterpillars, and the birds themselves may be eaten by cats. However, the caterpillars are also eaten by other insects, so most food chains are not so simple. Several linked chains make up a food web.

FOOD WEB

This diagram shows a food web based on the plants and trees in a small forest. A food web is much more complicated than a simple food chain, in which each plant or animal provides food for just one other animal. The plants provide food for many insects, worms, and other small animals, which in turn provide food for larger animals, such as cats, moles, and many different types of birds.

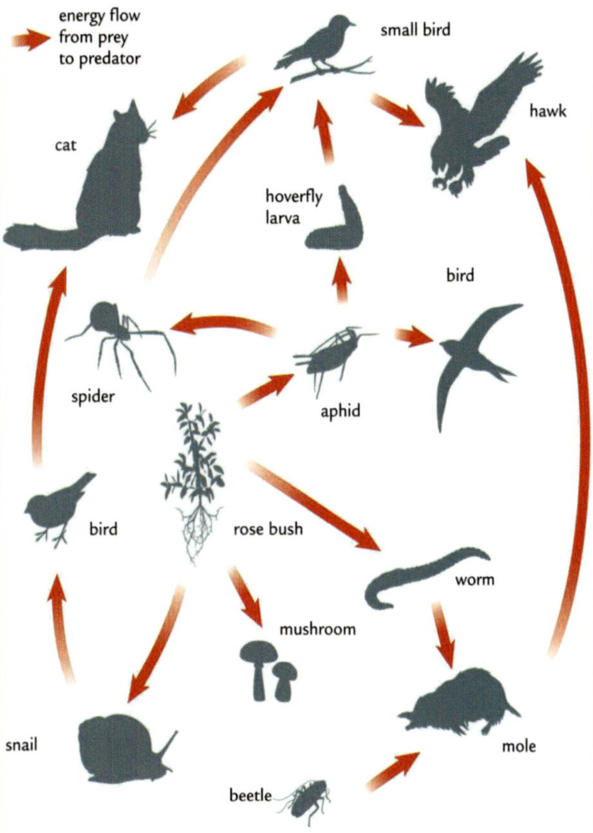

Suitable Habitats

All animals, plants, and other living organisms are involved in the "survival of the fittest." Many organisms die while the best adapted live to reproduce, a process called natural selection, which is the basis of evolution. The meaning of "fittest" depends on the environment. A goldfish can survive well in a pond, but it would die in a desert. A lizard can live in a desert, but it would freeze in the Arctic. Even if an animal or plant survives, it may not do as well as its neighbors. So over time it is crowded out.

STUDY A FOOD WEB

Make a list of all the animals that live in your backyard or in a local park. Remember to include insects and other mini-beasts, and all the animals with fur, feathers, or scales. Check out the animals in a book to see what they eat. Then try to arrange them in a food web like the one shown on page 7. It might get complicated!

EFFECTS ON PLANTS AND ANIMALS

By figuring out the relationships between plants and animals and their environment, an ecologist can try to predict what will happen if one part of the network is taken away. For example, if there is a plan to drain a mosquito-infested swamp, an ecologist can find out what other animals live in the swamp and how they might be affected. It may turn out that draining the swamp could destroy some rare and beautiful waterbirds.

↑ Alligators living in marshland could be affected if other animals or plants are removed from their habitat. Every organism plays an important role in an ecosystem.

Every living organism has characteristics, or adaptations, that make it suited to its own particular environment. The place in which an animal or plant lives is called its habitat.

A habitat could be a rocky seashore or a tropical forest. Such places offer all kinds of ways in which animals and plants can live. Every species of living organism has a special way of surviving in its habitat, and that is called its niche. For example, some birds specialize in eating large fruits, while others feed on small insects. The two types of birds occupy different niches.

Making a Community

A niche can be occupied by just one species. A small lake may have only enough food for one big predatory

POPULATIONS AND COMMUNITIES

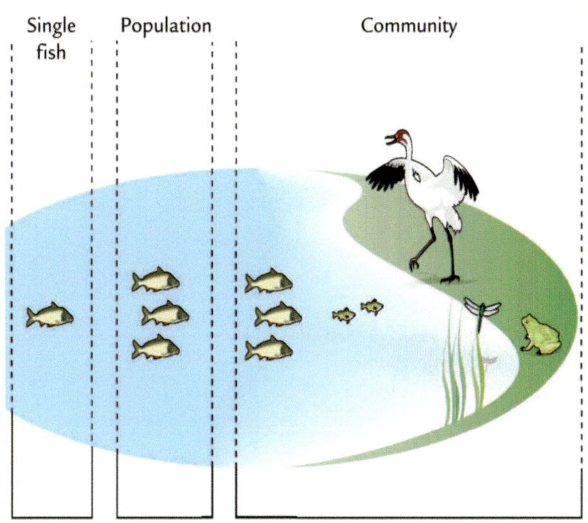

A river might be slow and muddy or swift and clear. The possibilities of the environment are endless. Communities of living organisms interact with their nonliving environment in all kinds of ways. These interactions often control the types of living things present in the community. For example, most riverside plants cannot grow in an estuary (where the tide mixes with freshwater) because the water is too salty.

fish, such as a pike, but a large lake will contain enough food for several pike, and they form a population. All the animals in a population are of the same species and occupy the same ecological niche. They share their lives with other populations of different animals and plants, and together these interacting populations form a community. So the fish, insects, birds, and plants in a lake make up a community.

What Are Ecosystems?

An ecological community can contain plants, animals, fungi, and microorganisms, such as bacteria. These living organisms share an environment that has nonliving elements, such as the climate (the typical weather experienced over a year), the soil, and the location, which might be an exposed, rocky headland or a sheltered, sandy beach.

MAKE YOUR OWN ECOSYSTEM

Create your own mini-ecosystem in a big glass jar by collecting some water from a pond in summer. Tell an adult before you go, and take care not to fall in! Fill your jar about three-quarters full. Then add some mud taken from the bottom of the pond. A layer one to two fingers thick should be enough. Add some water plants to the jar to produce oxygen. You can get them from the pond or from pet stores. Put your jar beside a window away from heat, and wait for a while. The water will clear, and you may be surprised at what you can see. The plants and animals will keep each other healthy for a period of time. Return all the organisms safely to the pond after you have looked at them.

MICROHABITATS AND COMMUNITIES

Most habitats are made of smaller microhabitats, such as the forest floor, a hole in a tree, or different layers of a tree. A forest usually has many different types of trees, and each tree can support its own community of animals. Different communities also live at different levels of the forest. One community lives on the forest floor, another in the understory, and yet another among the branches of the forest (top canopy, or branchy layer). Tropical forests have two or three canopy layers. More layers produce more communities. More communities create greater biodiversity (range of life-forms).

Only salt-tolerant plants can grow in estuary shallows. Along with the animals that live among them, these plants form a salt-marsh community. The cycle of complex interactions between the community and its environment is called an ecosystem.

What Are Biomes?

Any community in its environment is an ecosystem if it looks after itself. A pond is an ecosystem because all the animals and plants in it get almost everything they need without leaving the water. The plants make the oxygen and food that animals need; in turn the animals make the nutrients and carbon dioxide the plants need. Forests are also ecosystems. In some parts of the world forests cover vast areas. So do grasslands, oceans, and deserts. A large geographical region with its own distinctive climate, plants, and animals is called a biome and is generally made of several types of ecosystems. All the deserts on Earth are one biome; all tropical forests are another.

WHAT IS BIODIVERSITY?

Some ecological communities contain very few different species, usually because the habitat is difficult to live in. Arctic communities contain a much smaller range of species than rain forest communities. They have reduced biodiversity (variety of life). However, biodiversity can also change over time. If a wild prairie is turned into a giant wheatfield, its biodiversity goes down. Nearly all the wild plants disappear, and most of the animals that used to eat them vanish, too. Ecologists use biodiversity as a way of measuring how habitats are affected by land use.

The San Francisco Bay National Wildlife Refuge has a high biodiversity because it contains many different types of plant and animal species. These species include harbor seals, salt-marsh harvest mice, peregrine falcons, and pelicans.

CHAPTER 2

The Cycles of Nature

A life cycle is a series of stages a living thing goes through during its lifetime. The cycles of nature are powered by the sun and the raw materials of life are constantly recycled.

All living organisms need energy to grow and reproduce. Most of this energy comes from the sun. The energy is absorbed by plants, which use some of it to make energy-storing foods such as starch in a process called photosynthesis.

Herbivorous (plant-eating) animals, such as rabbits, eat plants and use the stored energy to power their own bodies. They also store some of the energy. If the rabbits are eaten by carnivores (meat eaters), such as foxes, the stored energy is passed on once again.

Plants that produce food using the sun's energy are producers. Animals that get their energy by eating are

← Plant-eating animals, such as this hare, gain their energy from plants, which, in turn, get their energy from the sun through the process of photosynthesis.

TOP OF THE FOOD CHAIN

A creature such as a bald eagle is at the very top energy level of its ecosystem. A single eagle pair needs to eat a lot of prey animals in order to support it. The prey, in turn, need to eat a huge number of plants to keep up their energy levels.

If anything interrupts the food supply lower down the ecosystem, the eagles are the first to run out of food and leave the area. So eagles and similar large predators are indicator species; that is, they show if the ecosystem is healthy.

consumers. All consumers rely on the producers lower down the food chain. In a meadow these producers might be grass plants. There are usually many levels of consumers—the grass may be eaten by rabbits, which are then eaten by foxes, which, in turn, may be eaten by eagles.

At each level energy is used up or lost. The total weight (or biomass; the total amount of living material) of grass eaten by rabbits is not all turned into rabbit flesh. Much of it is used up by hopping around and other activities. Only a small amount is stored and animal digestion is imperfect so does not make use of all the energy from food. It takes a lot of grass to support a colony of rabbits and a lot of rabbits to support a family of foxes.

WHAT ARE TROPHIC LEVELS?

Foxes and hawks both eat rabbits, but usually they do not eat each other. Ecologists say foxes and hawks are in the same trophic level in an ecosystem. Rabbits and mice eat grass and clover, which are on the trophic level below them. As a result of energy losses, the biomass of each ecosystem level is about one-tenth that of the level below. So, 2,200 pounds (1,000 kg) of grass and clover support 220 pounds (100 kg) of rabbits and mice but only 22 pounds (10 kg) of foxes and hawks. Thus there are many more rabbits than foxes in an ecosystem.

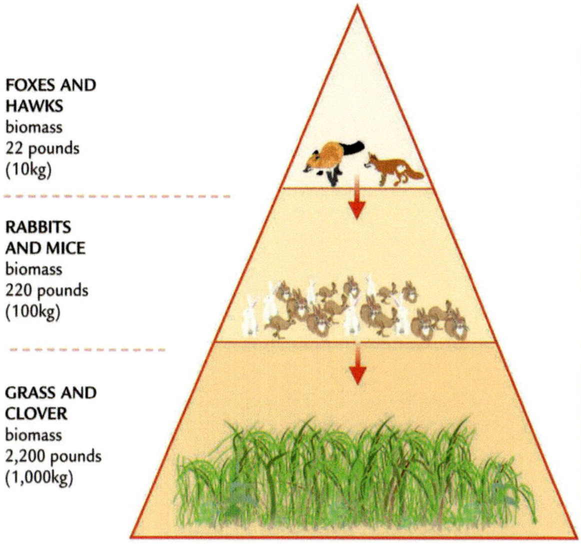

THE WEIGHT CONNECTION

Look at the food web on page 7. Which animals are not eaten by others and are at the top trophic level? Look up their weight in a book. Assume there are two of each, and add up their weights to get their biomass. Then arrange all the other animals in trophic levels, and figure out their biomass, remembering that each level weighs about 10 times the amount of the one above it. The weight at the bottom of the pyramid should be a lot more than it is at the top!

BREAKING DOWN A HIGH-FIBER DIET

If you find a snail in your backyard and put it in a tank with an empty jelly jar, it can eat the jar's paper label. The paper is made of cellulose, or plant fiber, and snails are among the few animals that can digest cellulose without help and turn it into sugar. Other animals, such as cows, have millions of bacteria in their stomachs that do the same job. In the process they produce a lot of a carbon-containing gas called methane, which passes back into the air to rejoin the carbon cycle.

THE CARBON CYCLE

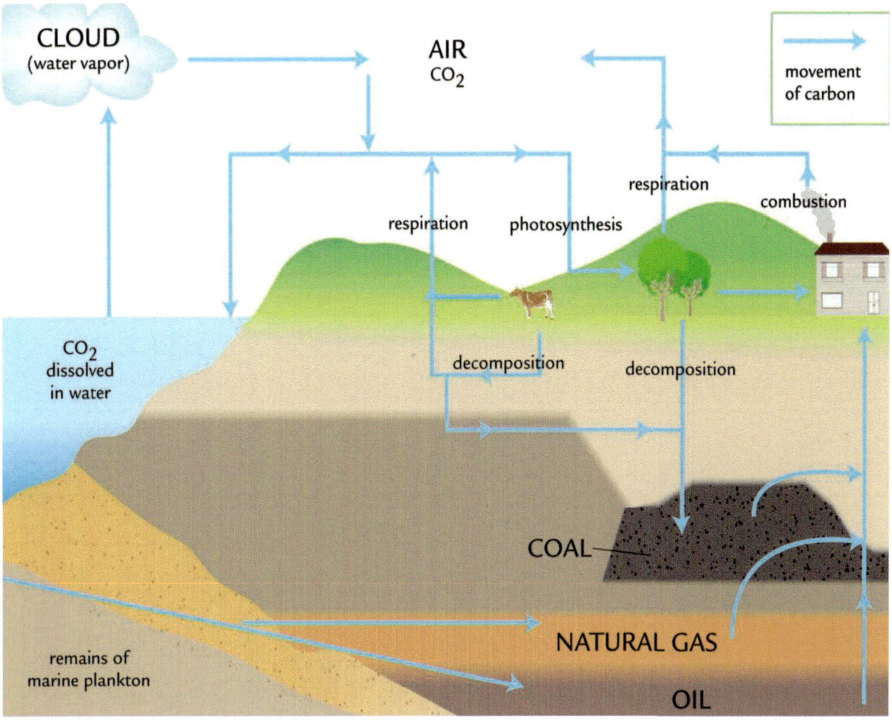

The carbon cycle shows how carbon moves around Earth. Plants take carbon dioxide from the atmosphere in photosynthesis and return it during the processes of respiration and decomposition. Over many years some carbon is kept away from the cycle by dead organisms that form deposits of rocks and fossil fuels. Later it goes back into the cycle during weathering of the rocks or burning of the fossil fuels.

What Is the Carbon Cycle?

The sun is a virtually limitless source of energy. However, the raw materials of life are not limitless and are constantly recycled. One of the most important materials is carbon, the element that is the main ingredient of oil, soot, and diamonds. Carbon has a special ability to combine with other elements to make molecules of different substances, including plant and animal tissues.

Plants get carbon from carbon dioxide gas in the air. They also take in water, which is made of hydrogen and oxygen. They use the sun's energy to combine carbon, hydrogen, and oxygen into

CREATING FOSSIL FUELS

When plants and animals die, the carbon in their bodies is usually recycled by other organisms and returned to the atmosphere (air around Earth). This recycling happens as the tissues decay or are broken down by microorganisms, such as bacteria. If these microorganisms cannot act on the tissues, after compression the remains become fossilized as carbon-rich coal or oil. The energy locked up in these tissues is also fossilized. If these fossil fuels are burned, the chemical reaction releases both the stored energy and the carbon, which returns to the air as carbon dioxide.

The huge quantities of fossil fuels burned over the last 150 years have released carbon that has been stored for millions of years. This activity has increased the amount of carbon dioxide in the atmosphere. Carbon dioxide is a greenhouse gas. It is the main cause of global warming (the increase in Earth's average air temperature), which is causing huge problems worldwide.

THE NITROGEN CYCLE

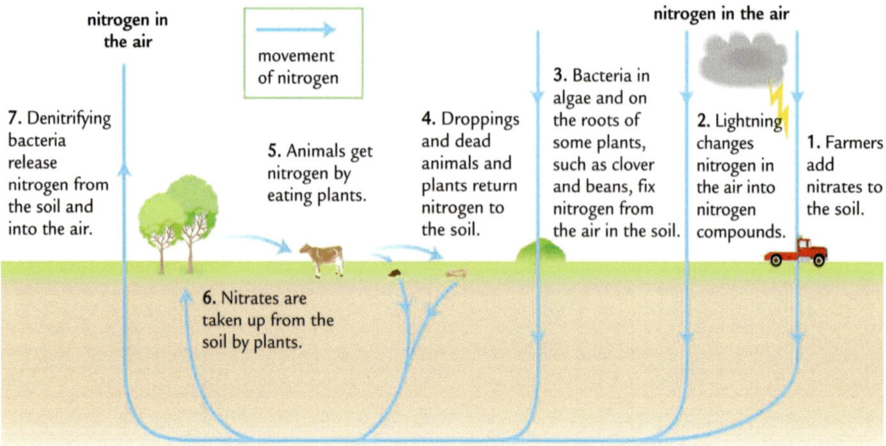

↑ The way nitrogen moves around Earth is called the nitrogen cycle. Plants and animals use nitrogen after it is chemically changed into nitrates by bacteria. Nitrogen returns to the soil when animals and plants die and by the addition of manure to soil. Denitrifying bacteria release nitrogen into the air again.

compounds called carbohydrates, substances such as sugar and starch, which store the sun's energy. Plants use sugars to fuel cell activities or store starch. They also use sugar to make a tough plant fiber called cellulose, the main part of plant tissue.

Plant By-Product

Plant-eating animals digest the sugar and starch in plants and change them into a sugar called glucose. They use it to build their own tissues and as an energy-rich fuel.

CONVERTING TO CARBON

Water plants gather carbon from carbon dioxide dissolved in water. If you put a pondweed such as Elodea in a glass jar of water and put the jar in bright sunlight, you will see small bubbles forming on the leaves. The bubbles are pure oxygen, which is released as the plant changes carbon dioxide and water into sugar.

THE USES OF FERTILIZER

Animal dung is made up of half-digested food remains mixed with a lot of digestive juices and bacteria. Once it is on the ground it decays quickly, releasing nitrogen compounds that can be taken up by plants. This action is part of the natural nitrogen cycle. Farmers can take advantage of it by spreading farmyard manure on their fields. As the manure breaks down, it adds nitrogen compounds and other nutrients, such as phosphorus and potassium, to the soil. They make the soil more fertile (rich in nutrients), so farm crops grow better. Farmers can also use fertilizer made in a factory, which contains nitrogen, phosphorus, and potassium. The chemical abbreviations for these elements are N, P, and K, so it is often called NPK fertilizer.

By combining the sugar with oxygen, which they get by breathing, plants change it back into carbon dioxide and water. This chemical reaction, called respiration, releases all the energy that the plants soaked up from the sun. The animals breathe out the carbon dioxide into the atmosphere, where it is available to the plants again.

The Nitrogen Cycle

Carbon is a vital part of living tissue because it can combine with other elements to make complex molecules. One of the most important of these elements is nitrogen, which links with carbon, hydrogen, and oxygen to form proteins. Proteins are the main building blocks of animal tissue, and they are also important to plants.

Nitrogen gas makes up 78 percent of the air, but it does not combine easily with other substances. That makes nitrogen almost useless to plants and animals in its raw state. However, in a process called nitrogen fixation some microorganisms turn nitrogen into compounds that are used by plants and can be turned into plant tissue.

A CLOSER LOOK AT ROOTS

Try growing some pea plants in pots. They sprout easily because each seed contains a lot of stored energy and protein. Eventually, however, they have to absorb extra nutrients through their roots. If you dig up a pea plant when it is tall, you will find tiny nodules (bumps) on its roots. They contain the bacteria that gather nitrogen from air in the soil and turn it into a form the plant can use.

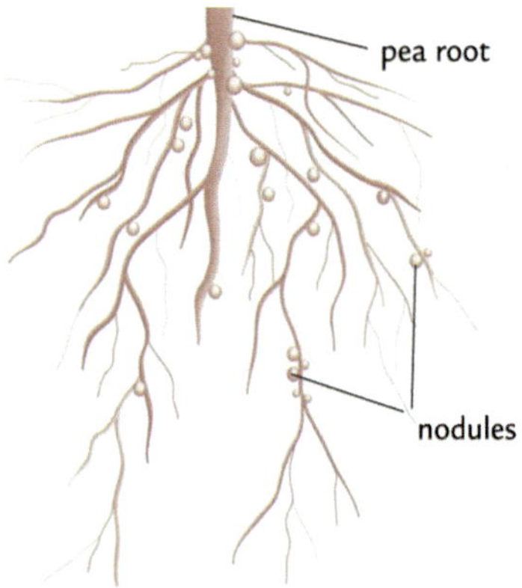

NITRATES AND THE ENVIRONMENT

The factory-made fertilizers used by farmers contain nitrogen in a form called nitrate, which is ideal for use by plants. That makes it instantly effective, unlike farmyard manure, which has to be broken down to nitrate by soil bacteria. However, nitrate dissolves in water, which is how the plants absorb it.

During wet weather the nitrates wash off the fields and into ponds and rivers. They then fertilize the water, which causes a massive growth of microscopic plantlike algae. This process upsets the aquatic ecosystem, and so there is a lot of debate about the use of factory-made nitrate fertilizers on land.

These microorganisms include bacteria that live in the soil and on the roots of plants such as clover and beans.

Breaking Down Plant Matter

Plants use nitrogen to build proteins. When animals eat plants or each other, they digest the proteins and use their ingredients to make new proteins. When plants and animals die, bacteria and other microorganisms attack the proteins and break them down, releasing nitrogen compounds into the soil. The plants can absorb these types of compounds into their roots with water and recycle them to make more plant proteins.

BIRDS AND GUANO

Fish are the main food for millions of ocean birds, which breed on coasts and islands. These breeding sites become smothered in bird dung (guano). Guano is rich in phosphorus because of all the fish bones swallowed by the birds.

On some sites the guano has built up over thousands of years to form thick layers. In the nineteenth century these ancient guano deposits were mined to make phosphorus-rich fertilizer for spreading over farm crops.

Bird guano covers these rocks in Paracas national reserve on Peru's south coast.

ANIMALS AND MINERALS

Animals need some mineral nutrients that plants do not. These minerals include sodium, an ingredient in table salt. Since most plants do not need sodium, they do not absorb it. Thus, plant-eating animals may not get any sodium in their diet. They often deal with the problem by licking the mineral from rocks or soil that contain sodium. In Peru, macaws and other birds visit clay-licks, steep walls of clay caused by erosion along riverbanks, to get mineral supplements. The minerals may also neutralize the effects of toxic fruits and seeds the birds eat.

What Is the Phosphorus Cycle?

Carbon and nitrogen exist in gases in the atmosphere, but other raw materials of life, such as phosphorus, potassium, calcium, and sodium, are normally solid minerals or dissolved in water.

Phosphorus is essential to living things. It is a vital ingredient of nucleic acids, such as DNA. Plants need phosphorus for healthy root growth, while animals use phosphorus and calcium to form teeth and bones. Both minerals occur in rocks. When rocks are weathered into mineral grains, they become part of the soil. Plants take them up in soil water and build them into their tissues. That makes phosphorus and calcium available to plant-eating animals and, in turn, to meat-eating animals. When plants and animals die, their tissues decay, and so the phosphorus and other nutrients pass back into the soil.

EXPLORING THE CYCLE

Simple nutrients like carbon, nitrogen, and phosphorus are constantly cycling around the global ecosystem. Some, such as nitrogen, cycle quickly. Others, such as the carbon in fossil fuels, cycle over millions of years. Since everything cycles around eventually, does it matter how these substances are used? Does it matter, for example, if people burn a lot of coal and oil and release a lot of carbon dioxide into the atmosphere?

Rock Breakdown

As rainwater drains through soil and into small streams, it carries with it nutrients, such as phosphorus, calcium, and other minerals. The streams drain into rivers that flow to the sea. Thus these minerals become available to aquatic animals, such as fish. When the fish die, their remains drift to the ocean floor, where the minerals gradually build up in layers that turn into solid rock. After millions of years the rock may be pushed to the surface and eventually form more soil.

CHAPTER 3

Climates on Earth

Each place on Earth has its own climate, a regular pattern of weather. The amount of sun, rain, and wind determines the types of plants that can grow in an area. This, in turn, affects the animal species that live there.

Palm trees bend under the force of powerful winds called hurricanes, which blow at more than 75 miles per hour (120 km/h). Hurricanes start above ocean areas in the tropics.

Climate is a broad picture of the average weather conditions experienced in a region over many years. The sun provides the energy that drives the weather and so produces climate. It causes winds to blow and moisture to circulate between the atmosphere and the surface of Earth in a continual process called the water cycle. All the day-to-day weather conditions, such as sunshine, showers, storms, and blizzards, are caused by the sun heating various parts of Earth by different amounts. Differences in

EFFECTS OF THE SUN

The sun's rays travel in parallel lines toward Earth. They strike down from directly above at the equator, where they are concentrated on a relatively small area. The climate in the tropics is always hot. The sun beats down less directly in temperate regions, which are north and south of the tropics, so they have a cooler climate. At the polar regions, where Earth's surface is most curved, the rays strike at a sharp (oblique) angle and are spread out over a much wider area. The rays also have farther to travel through the atmosphere, which absorbs heat, so the polar climate is cold.

temperature produce variations in air pressure, the force exerted on Earth's surface by the weight of the air around it. Changes in air pressure then cause air masses to move from one place to another, which produces winds. Winds may bring warm or cool temperatures and dry or rainy spells.

Factors That Affect the Climate

The three main factors influencing climate are latitude (distance from the equator), altitude (height above sea level), and how far a region is from the sea.

CLIMATES AROUND THE WORLD

Austrian scientist Wladimir Köppen (1846–1940) was among the first people to classify regions according to climate. Köppen studied how climate affects plant life in different parts of the world. In 1918 he produced a classification listing five main climate zones: tropical/rainy; dry; temperate/rainy; cold/snowy; and polar. Köppen's classification is still used today, but many modern climatologists (climate experts) distinguish at least a dozen climate zones, as shown on the map below.

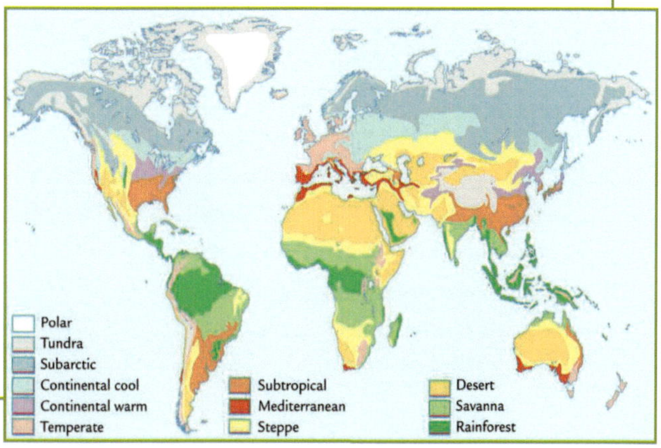

THE SEASONS

The tilting of Earth on its axis as it goes around the sun means that the northern hemisphere is tipped closer to the sun in June, making longer and warmer days in the season called summer.

In June the southern hemisphere is tipped farther from the sun, causing the winter, a season with colder and shorter days. The opposite happens in December.

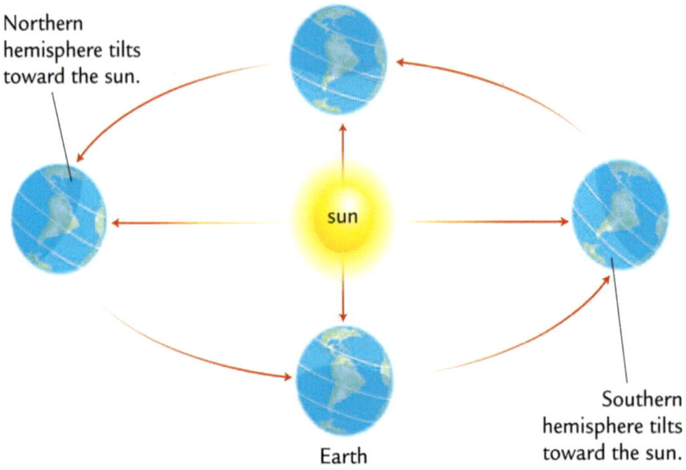

Latitude is a very important factor. Earth's curving surface enables various regions to receive differing amounts of the sun's heat.

Earth and the Seasons

Many parts of the world experience regular seasonal changes because Earth tilts on its axis (an imaginary line linking the North and South poles) at an angle of 23.5° as it orbits the sun. At any time one hemisphere (half of Earth) leans toward the sun and has summer with long hours of daylight. The other hemisphere tilts away and has winter with short days.

KEEP A RECORD OF THE SEASONS

Monitor how seasonal changes affect the area where you live by keeping records. Record temperatures at regular times each day for one week each month, and note the hours of daylight. You could also record how the seasons affect local plants and animal behavior. For example, local mammals and reptiles may not be seen in winter because they hibernate, and some local birds may migrate.

Seasonal changes are least noticeable in the tropics, which is the regions closest to the equator that always face the sun. However, some parts of the tropics have a dry and a rainy season. Many temperate regions have four seasons: spring, summer, fall, and winter. The poles have the greatest variation in temperature and day length. For part of the summer each pole is bathed in weak sunlight for 24 hours a day. For part of the winter the sun never rises. Arctic plants cope with this by becoming dormant (inactive) in winter. Many animals hibernate (enter a sleeplike state) or migrate (move away) to avoid the cold.

Altitude and the Weather

Height above sea level, or altitude, also affects a region's climate because the thinner air at higher altitudes absorbs less of the sun's heat. The temperature drops about 5.4°F for every 1,000 feet (305 m) climbed. Mountain climates are thus much cooler than the surrounding lowlands, with shorter

MOUNTAIN CLIMATES

Altitude affects the types of plants that grow at different heights on mountains. Generally, only small plants grow higher up on mountains. Broad-leaved trees such as oaks may grow at a mountain's base, but only cold-resistant conifers, such as pine trees, thrive higher up.

Even higher, beyond a zone called the tree line, there are no trees, only low-growing plants. The kinds of plants that can grow at that altitude are usually found in alpine tundra regions. No vegetation grows beyond the snow line because the climate there is too harsh.

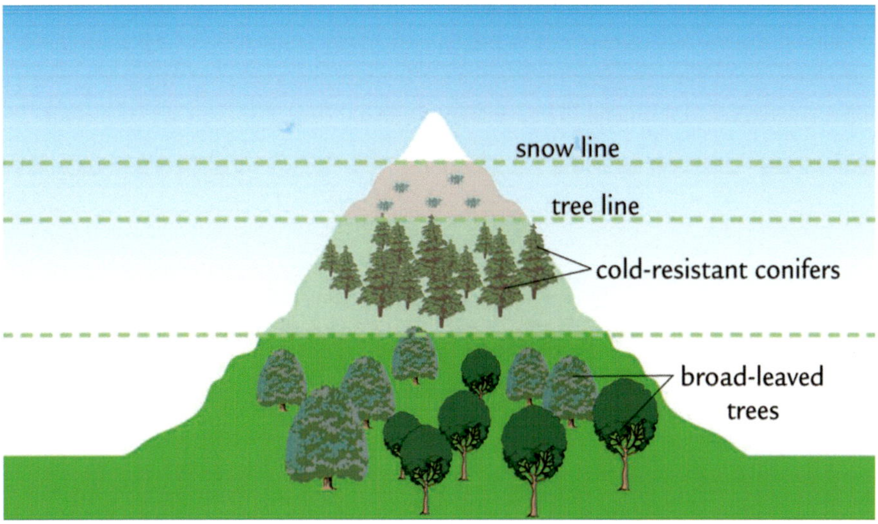

Kilimanjaro, the tallest mountain in Africa, is 19,340 feet (5,895 m) at its highest point. Although it is just a few miles from the equator, it is always capped by snow because temperature falls with thinner air at increasing altitude.

summers and longer winters. The tops of high mountains near the equator, such as Kilimanjaro in East Africa, are always covered with snow.

Climate on Sea and Land

Distance from the sea also affects a region's climate. The oceans absorb the sun's heat more slowly than the land but retain their warmth longer. Coasts may also be warmed or cooled by ocean currents and are thus usually milder than regions far inland and also wetter because winds blowing inshore off the sea are laden with moisture. Coastal regions have a maritime climate, while areas far inland have a continental climate.

The Atmosphere

The atmosphere is a blanket of gases surrounding Earth like the peel on an orange. It extends about 450 miles (720 km) into space. The main gases in the atmosphere

The cloud formation on the coastline of a beach in Kauai, Hawaii, is typical of a maritime climate.

THE LAYERS OF THE ATMOSPHERE

About 75 percent of the air in the atmosphere exists below 6.5 miles (10.5 km). The air is progressively thinner closer to space. There are five main layers in the atmosphere. The lowest layer, the troposphere, extends to 12 miles (19 km) above the planet's surface. Most weather occurs here. Above that is a calm layer, the stratosphere, extending to about 30 miles (48 km) up. Aircraft fly there to avoid turbulence. Most meteors burn up in the layer beyond, the mesosphere, 30 to 50 miles (48–80 km) up. The thermosphere (50 to 280 miles, 80–450 km, up) contains electrically charged particles. Beyond is the exosphere, a thin layer extending into space.

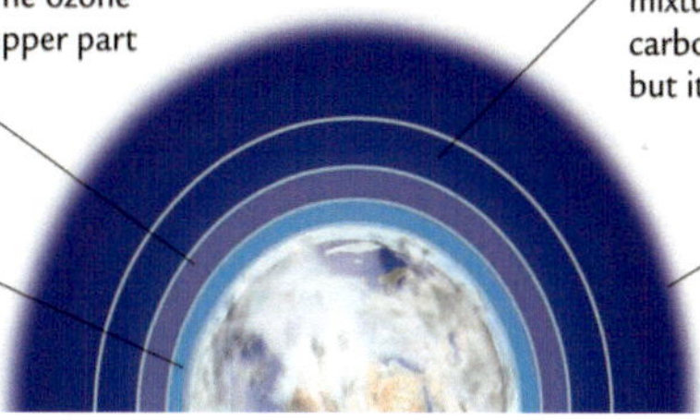

are nitrogen (78 percent) and oxygen (21 percent). Smaller amounts of carbon dioxide, water vapor, nitrous oxide, ozone, and other gases are also present. They are important because they trap the sun's warmth. The atmosphere shields Earth from harmful radiation, keeps out the cold of space, and contains oxygen for living things to breathe. Without it life on Earth would be impossible.

The Ozone Layer

A layer of ozone gas is present in the stratosphere about 15 miles (24 km)

LOSS OF THE OZONE LAYER

In the 1980s scientists discovered that a hole in the atmosphere containing less ozone than normal was appearing over Antarctica each spring. During the 1990s ozone holes over Antarctica and the Arctic became steadily bigger. Scientists showed that chlorofluorocarbons (CFCs) were mainly causing the damage. CFCs are chemicals used in the manufacture of refrigerators, polystyrene packaging, and aerosol spray cans, and in air conditioning. The loss of ozone has caused an increase in skin cancer in people and animals in recent years.

Refrigerators containing CFCs threatened the ozone layer. CFCs were replaced by safer gases.

EFFECTS ON SEA LEVEL

During the last main ice age, sea levels were about 400 feet (120 m) lower than today. As the glaciers and ice caps melted, the levels rose and flooded great areas of dry land. Global warming may do this but in a fraction of the time, centuries rather than millennia.

The diagrams below show (**a**) the position of Florida's coastline 18,000 years ago, when the sea level was lower than present, and (**b**) and (**c**) the possible situation if global warming causes the polar ice cap to melt. Most of Florida would disappear completely.

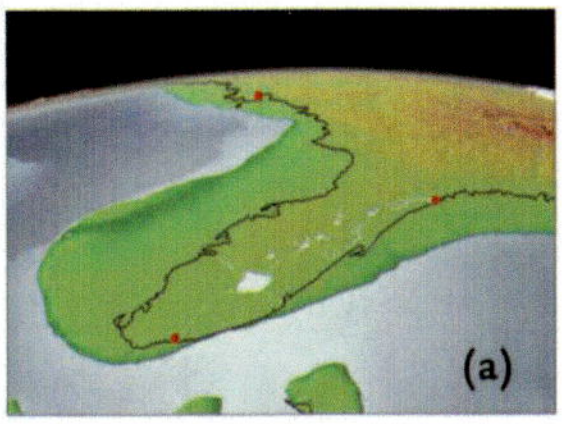

(a)

Sea level 18,000 years ago, 394 feet (120 m) lower than present.

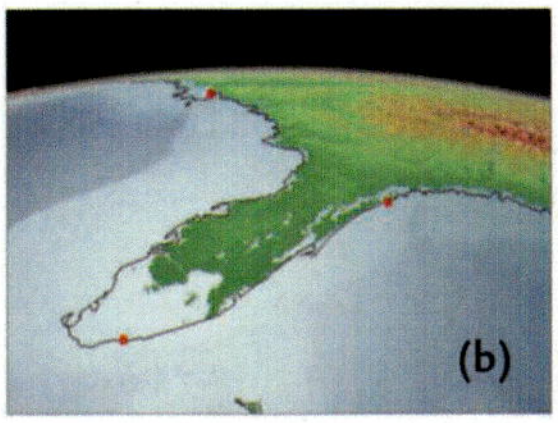

(b)

Possible future sea level 17 feet (5 m) higher than present.

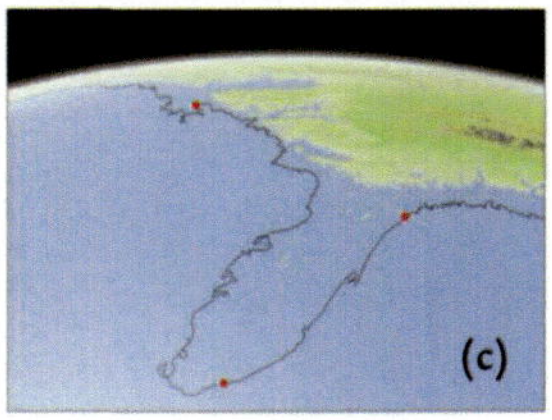

(c)

Possible future sea level 170 feet (50 m) higher than present.

above Earth's surface. Ozone, a form of oxygen, is a bluish gas. The ozone layer shields Earth from harmful ultraviolet (UV) radiation in sunlight. UV rays can cause illnesses such as cancer and eye damage in animals and also harm plants, including phytoplankton, a major food source in the sea.

Greenhouse Effect

Carbon dioxide, methane, water vapor, and other gases in the atmosphere act as a barrier that traps heat rising from Earth's surface and

A MINI- ICE AGE

Between about 1400 and 1800 Earth had a mini-ice age. Winters were much colder than they are now. Rivers and lakes froze over regularly and ice fairs were held on the ice. During the last ice fair on the Thames River in London in 1814 (below) the thick ice supported the weight of an elephant. Landscapes by European artists showing frozen waterways in winter were once a common sight.

WHAT IS GLOBAL WARMING?

In the last 200 years Earth's climate has been growing steadily warmer in a process called global warming. Temperatures rose by 1°F (0.5 °C) in the last 50 years and may now be rising more rapidly. Scientists have found that human-made pollution is causing the warming. As people burn more and more fossil fuels in cars, power plants, homes, and factories, increasing amounts of carbon dioxide is added to the atmosphere, which in turn increases the rate of global warming.

A CLOSER LOOK AT TREE RINGS

Studying tree rings provides information about climate. Trees produce these trunk rings as they add new layers of wood beneath the bark each year during the growing season.

Find a tree that has been cut down, and study the tree rings to find out about climate during the tree's lifetime. The newest rings are on the outside, with the oldest growth near the center. Find the wide, light rings, which represent the spring and summer seasons, when the tree was growing at its quickest. A narrower dark ring, representing winter growth, separates these wider rings.

Count inwards from the outer bark to find out when these rings occurred (one year for each light ring). You can also count all the rings to find out the tree's age when it was cut down. Some bristlecone pines in the western United States are 4,000 years old.

prevents it from escaping into space. These gases have a similar effect as the glass in a greenhouse, so this process is called the greenhouse effect. For millions of years the greenhouse effect has created a warm environment on Earth that has allowed living organisms to flourish there. However, scientists now know that human-made pollution is having an increasing effect on Earth's greenhouse gases and causing temperatures to rise above normal, an effect called global warming. One result of this is the gradual melting of the polar ice, which is threatening the animals that live there and causing oceans to flood coastal land.

WHAT IS THE WATER CYCLE?

Moisture moves constantly between the air, land, and oceans in a process called the water cycle. The sun's heat causes moisture from oceans, lakes, and wet ground to evaporate (turn into water vapor). At cooler temperatures the moisture condenses (turns into liquid) to form clouds, which later shed rain or snow. When rain falls, the excess moisture not absorbed by the soil or taken up by plants drains into streams, rivers, and lakes, which eventually empty into the ocean, and so the cycle goes around again.

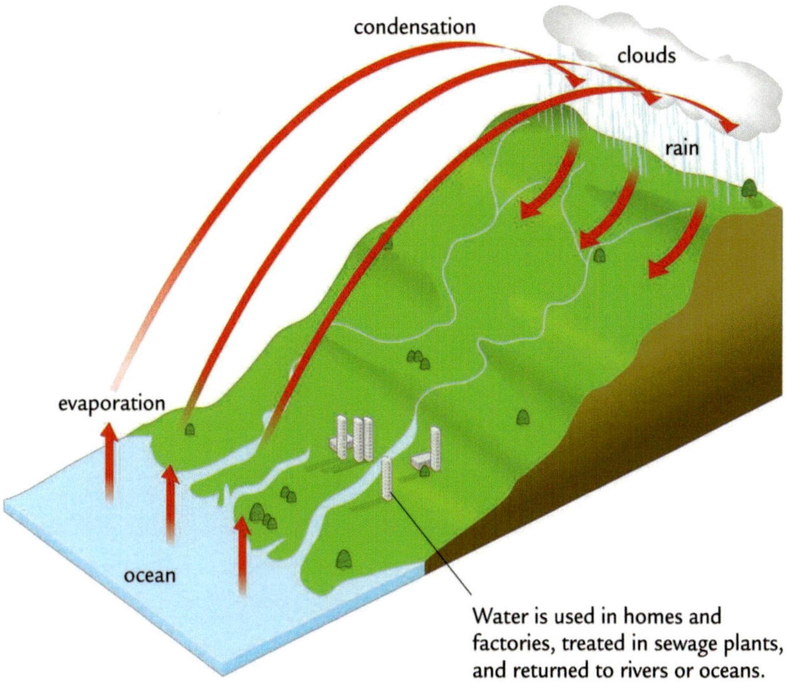

CHANGING BELIEFS ABOUT EROSION

Before 1800 most people believed that Earth was only a few thousand years old. A group of scientists called the Neptunists thought that all landforms had been shaped by a series of disasters in the distant past and had not changed since then. Scotsman Dr. James Hutton (1726–1797) was among the first to say that Earth was much older—millions rather than thousands of years old. Hutton rightly believed that natural forces such as waves, wind, and water were continually shaping Earth.

SOIL HORIZONS

Scientists distinguish several different layers called horizons in a vertical slice of soil, called a soil profile (right). The depth of each layer varies with the type of soil. The topmost layer (horizon O) is a rich layer of humus made of plant and animal remains. Below that the topsoil (horizon A) is a dark, fertile layer containing humus. The subsoil (horizon B) is nourished by minerals washed from the topsoil. The zone of partly weathered rock below that (horizon C) is less fertile. Last comes the bedrock (horizon D or R), the source of the minerals in the soil.

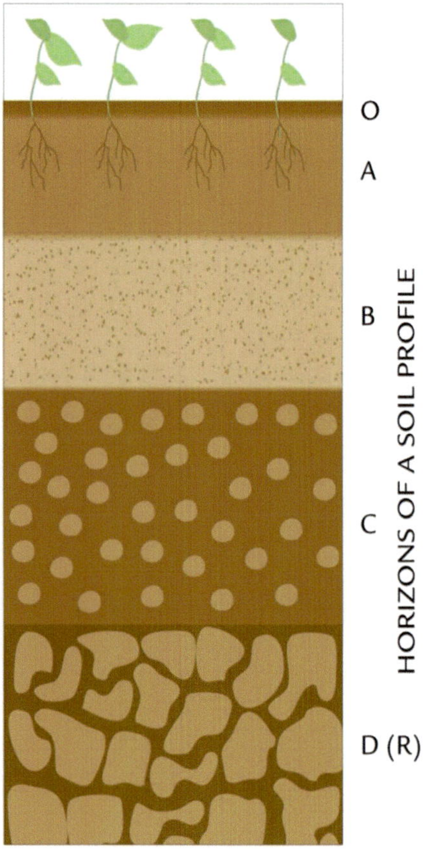

WATER PRESERVATION

The world's rainfall is not evenly distributed over the planet's surface. Some regions receive high rainfall, while in deserts rain may not fall for many years. Where water is scarce, people may have to spend hours every day just traveling to fetch enough water to meet their needs. Elsewhere supplies may be plentiful, but purifying and distributing it still uses up energy and costs money. Do you think it is important to try and save water? If so, can you think how it can be done?

Long-Term Climate Change

Earth's climate appears to stay the same, but it changes very slowly. Long, cold periods called ice ages gradually give way to warmer ones. Scientists believe these long-term changes are caused because Earth wobbles slightly as it orbits the sun. During the past 2 million years a total of 15 ice ages have come and gone. The last major ice age ended about 10,000 years ago. During these cold periods ice covered large parts of what are now temperate regions, including much of North America and Europe.

Scientists find out about Earth's climate in the past using various techniques. In one method samples of ice buried deep in the polar regions are collected. Examination of these ice cores reveals what the climate was like many thousands of years ago, when snow fell to form the ice. Studying tree rings also yields information about climate.

As well as oxygen from the atmosphere, all organisms need water, which makes up on average 75 percent of living things. Water exists on Earth in three forms—as a liquid, as a gas (water vapor), and in solid form as ice. Moisture collects in the atmosphere to form clouds made up of millions of tiny water droplets. Clouds shed moisture as precipitation in the form of rain, hail, or snow.

The Soil and Climate Link

Soil forms the link between the living world and the nonliving rocks that make up Earth. Most living things on land need the soil either directly or indirectly to live. Plants root in the soil and take water and nourishment from it. An area of soil just 1 foot (30 cm) square may contain literally millions of organisms, including insects, spiders, slugs, and worms, and microscopic bacteria and fungi. Many of them help to break down plant and animal remains so their nutrients return to fertilize the soil.

Over thousands of years soil is slowly created by the forces of weather, as ice, frost, wind, and running water break down the rocks at Earth's surface in a process called erosion. Different types of soil, including chalk, clay, sand, and peat, are present in different regions. The type of soil depends on many factors, including climate, vegetation, and the composition of the underlying rock.

CHAPTER 4

What Are Ecosystems?

Ecosystems are identifiable units consisting of living things and their nonliving environment. An ecosystem can be as small as a tiny pond or as vast as the ocean.

A number of factors come together to make our planet suitable for life. Earth is just the right distance from the sun to receive the light and heat needed for life to flourish. The atmosphere protects us from harmful rays from space and contains life-giving oxygen. There is plenty of water, and the oceans as well as the atmosphere help to regulate temperatures. Earth has all the conditions needed to support life except an energy source, and that is provided by our local star, the sun. In contrast, Mars is too far from the sun to sustain life. The average temperatures there, -81°F (-63°C), are too cold for life, since the atmosphere is too thin to retain heat. Venus, closer to the sun than Earth, is too hot for life, with average temperatures of 864°F (262°C) and a thick, dense atmosphere of carbon dioxide. Mars and Venus also lack water to support life.

↑ Even a small pond in a canyon, such as this one in Colorado, is an ecosystem.

THE BIOSPHERE

The biosphere is all parts of Earth that are able to sustain life, including the atmosphere, oceans, the surface of the land, and just below it. This living layer extends from about 30,000 feet (9 km) in the air down to the ocean depths and to about 8 miles (13 km) below the land's surface, where microorganisms can survive. Above 30,000 feet the air is too thin to support life, while at depths greater than 8 miles the heat and the pressure are too great. Within this living layer most life exists in a much narrower band, which extends from the upper waters of the oceans to about 1,000 feet (300 m) up.

EXTREMOPHILES

Most life exists in a relatively narrow zone around the surface of the Earth, down into the soil, deep sea and sea-bed mud, and up a few miles (kilometers) into the air. This is the main part of the living world, or biosphere. However some living things, mostly microorganisms, can cope with extreme conditions of temperature, pressure, and nutrient lack, deep below polar ice caps or floating high in the troposphere. They are known as extremophiles.

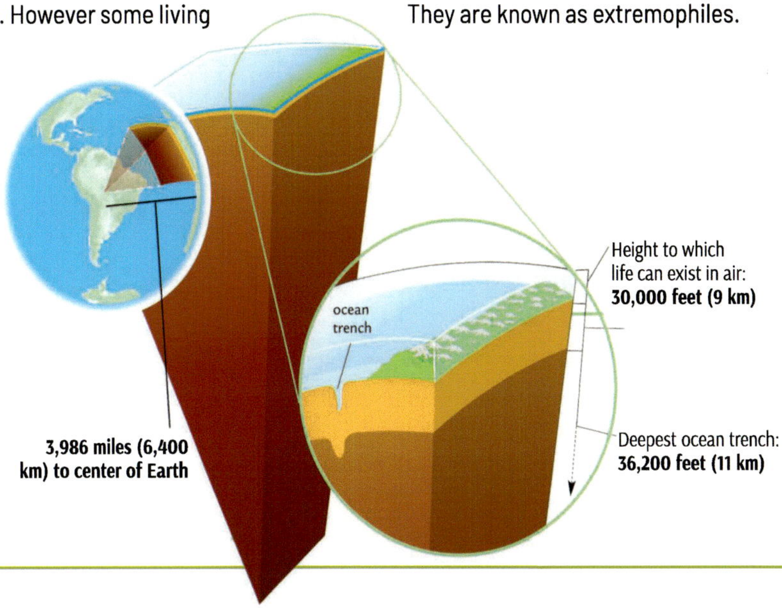

LOOK AT LOCAL ECOSYSTEMS

Make a map of the ecosystems in your local area by tracing or photocopying a large-scale aerial photograph. Now survey the area on foot, noting ecosystems such as woodlands, ponds, fields, built-up areas, and wasteland. You could also mark particular features such as a rabbit or gopher warren or a colony of nesting birds. Be very careful and ask an adult to go with you when you do the survey.

What Are Biomes?

Earth is divided into a number of huge ecosystems such as deserts, forests, tundra, and mountains. They fit together like the pieces of an enormous jigsaw puzzle. Each piece is a biome, with its own climate and distinctive soil, plants, and animals.

The climate, geography, and other factors allow certain types of vegetation to grow well. This in turn supports particular types of animals, fungi, and microscopic life.

Some biomes support vast numbers of living organisms, while other biomes are much less productive. Of the dry land that occupies about 30 percent of Earth's surface, one-third is desert, and another fifth is either tundra (treeless areas where the subsoil is frozen) or permanently covered with ice. These harsh biomes support relatively little life. Biomes such as forests, grasslands, and warm, shallow seas teem with life.

Polar Climates

The polar regions are the harshest places on Earth, with short, cold summers and long, dark, freezing winters. A desert is anywhere

↑ Polar bears live in the Arctic. To keep out the cold, they have thick fur and a layer of fat.

with less than 10 inches (25 cm) of rain every year, so polar regions are deserts because there is very little rainfall and almost no liquid water on the ground. The land is permanently covered by a thick cap of ice more than 2 miles (3.2 km) deep in places. The oceans are warmer but still frozen over for much of the year. Little life can survive on land in these bleak conditions; but the polar oceans, with their nutrient-rich currents, teem with life, from microscopic plankton to Earth's largest creatures, giant blue whales.

BREAKING DOWN THE WORLD'S BIOMES

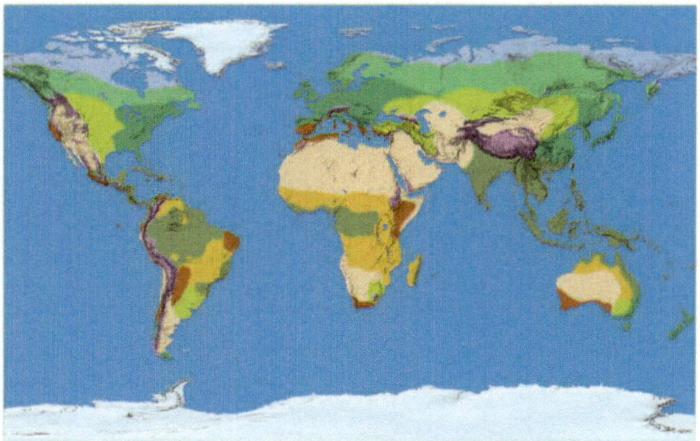

Biomes are large regions that have similar climate, plants, and animals. This map shows Earth's main land biomes: polar, tundra, mountain, desert, scrubland, grasslands, and forest. Forest biomes can be divided into cool, temperate, and tropical forests. Oceans and lakes offer saltwater and freshwater biomes. Each biome contains ecosystems with particular conditions. The distance from the equator is one factor that determines climate, so divisions between biomes broadly follow lines of latitude.

- Polar desert
- Arctic tundra
- Taiga
- Temperate forest
- Temperate grassland
- Desert and semidesert
- Shrubland
- Tropical grassland
- Tropical forest, including rain forest
- Mountain and highland
- Ocean

What Are Tundras?

The bleak, treeless lands that lie south of the arctic wastes are the tundra. There the climate is also harsh, with cool, brief summers and long, icy winters. Snow and ice cover the ground for much of the year, but in summer the snow melts to reveal grassy lowlands with bogs and lakes. Beneath the topsoil is a layer of permanently frozen ground called the permafrost in which trees cannot root.

However, low-growing shrubs, mosses, lichens, and flowering plants make the most of the short summer growing season. Few animals live all year on the tundra. Insects die in the fall, leaving their eggs or larvae

Mount Rainier and a summer alpine meadow in Mount Rainier National Park, Washington state. Mountain biomes vary from snowcapped peaks to temperate lower slopes, according to altitude.

(young) in the soil to hatch the following spring. Birds and mammals that live year round include arctic foxes, lemmings, and snowy owls. Many more, including caribou, geese, ducks, and seabirds, migrate to the tundra to breed in spring.

Mountain Climate

The effects of altitude on climate create mountain zones that contain several mini-biomes with conditions similar to those normally found over a huge north–south range. The summits of high mountains are permanently covered with snow and ice, like the polar regions. Below that is a bleak, treeless zone with vegetation similar to the tundra. Farther down, slopes may feature cool forest and temperate or tropical plant life, depending on the mountain's location.

STRUCTURES OF THE TUNDRA

The harsh climate of the tundra makes the building of houses, roads, and other structures difficult. Engineers encounter problems because of the underlying permafrost. If heat is transferred to the frozen ground through a structure's foundations, the soil may become boggy, causing the structure to sink. If the ground freezes and thaws repeatedly, ice may heave up buildings, causing cracking. Many structures are built on stilts to avoid such problems. The Trans-Alaska Pipeline, which transports oil from the arctic south across the tundra, is above the ground to stop the warm oil from melting the permafrost.

FARMING IN THE 1930s

In the 1930s bad farming practices turned a huge area of the American prairies into a barren wasteland. As the West was settled, farmers removed the natural vegetation to plant crops. Without grass roots to anchor the soil, year after year of drought reduced it to dust. High winds blew the dust away, creating a desert often called a dust bowl. The region's fertility was restored only after many years of careful management.

Grassland Climate

Grasslands cover roughly 19 million square miles (50 million sq km) worldwide—that is one-third of Earth's habitable land area. Most grasslands lie between desert biomes and tropical or temperate forests. There are two main types of grasslands: savannas, or tropical grasslands, and temperate grasslands. Tropical grasslands generally experience an annual dry and rainy season, and have scattered trees and shrubs. Temperate grasslands receive a more even distribution of yearly rainfall.

The major temperate grasslands of the world include the Central Asian steppes and the American prairies. Huge tracts of these vast grasslands have been plowed to grow crops such as wheat, corn, and oats.

Wild grasslands of the world are home to around 7,500 different species of grasses but relatively few trees. Grasslands are rich biomes that support huge numbers of insects and microorganisms, and a variety of birds and reptiles. Grassland mammals fall roughly into two main groups: burrowers and grazers. The burrowers include smaller ground squirrels and rabbits, while the grazers include larger animals such as antelope, zebras, and wildebeest.

Forest Climate

Forest biomes together cover a third of Earth's land area. There are three main types of forests: coniferous, deciduous, and tropical forest. Climate is the main factor that determines which type of forest grows.

A wide belt of coniferous forest called the taiga rings the northern hemisphere south of the tundra. Conifers such as spruce, larch, fir, and pine thrive in the harsh climate there, with bitterly cold winters and low rainfall. These cone-bearing trees have narrow, waxy leaves that minimize moisture loss and withstand cold well. All except larch are evergreen. The dense foliage throughout the year severely limits the amounts of both light and moisture that filter through to ground level, so plant and animal life is relatively sparse on the forest floor.

The world's temperate regions are generally characterized by warm summers, cool winters, and abundant rainfall. Here, forests of deciduous trees such as oak, beech, ash, and maple shed their leaves in fall to conserve moisture in winter, then grow new leaves in spring. For much of the year the bare branches allow abundant light and moisture to reach the ground, where wildlife thrives in the rich soil. In tropical areas with

an annual dry and rainy season trees also shed their leaves in the dry season.

Tropical rain forests grow in low-lying regions near the equator that receive more than 100 inches (250 cm) of rain a year. Vegetation thrives in these warm, wet conditions and supports an abundance of wildlife. Rain forests cover just 6 percent of Earth's land area, yet scientists estimate they host up to 70 percent of all living species. The world's largest rain

A deciduous, or seasonal, forest mostly made up of broad-leaved trees that shed their leaves in fall. This type of forest grows in temperate regions, which have warm summers and cool winters. The other two types of forests are coniferous and tropical.

THE PRODUCTS OF RAIN FORESTS

Tropical forests yield hundreds of products familiar in stores in developed countries. Perhaps the most obvious is hardwood timber, used to make furniture. As well as a wide range of fruits, nuts, and spices, tropical forests also yield sugar, coffee, palm oil, chocolate, rubber, and chicle, which is used to make chewing gum.

In addition, plants such as the rosy periwinkle from Madagascar are used to make medicines.

MAKING A RAIN FOREST

Make a mini-rain forest using an old fish tank or a large jar with a lid. Cover the base of the container with gravel, then add charcoal and a layer of compost. Plant tropical plants from a garden center in the soil, mist their leaves with a plant spray, and then replace the lid. The plants will recycle the moisture inside their mini-ecosystem, so you will not need to water them much.

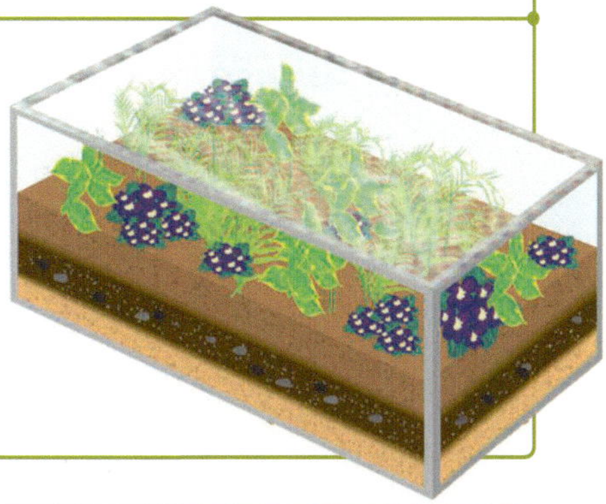

forest, the Amazon rain forest in South America, occupies a vast area. However tropical forests worldwide are disappearing at an alarming rate.

These Joshua trees, cacti, and desert grasses are commonly found in desert regions. These species grow particularly well after wet seasons.

Desert and Scrubland Climate

Deserts are defined as places where less than 10 inches (25 cm) of rain falls annually. Scrublands, often on the borders of deserts, are slightly wetter but still have a low rainfall. In low-lying deserts, such as the Sahara Desert in Africa, temperatures may climb to 130°F (54°C) by day but drop steeply at night. High deserts, such as the Gobi Desert in Central Asia, have an even harsher climate, with temperatures that drop below freezing at night.

ISLAND LIFE

The English naturalist Charles Darwin (1809–1882) visited the remote Galápagos Islands off Ecuador in the 1830s. His experiences there helped him formulate his ideas on evolution. He discovered many of the islands had their own species of birds called finches, with beaks specialized for different foods. Darwin speculated that all had evolved from a single species of finch that had reached the islands several hundred thousand years before.

Desert organisms have features that enable them to cope with the harsh conditions and particularly the lack of water. Many desert plants have a deep or extensive root system to gather moisture from the surrounding soil. Plants called succulents, such as cacti, store moisture in their fleshy leaves, stems, or roots. Many desert animals are active by night, when temperatures are cooler, and are able to withstand a period of drought.

Ecosystems in Urban Areas

As human populations grow and expand around the world, so more and more wild land is transformed into urban environments. For many species this change is disastrous, but some types of plants and animals have adapted to thrive in this new habitat. Opportunistic feeders such as raccoons and foxes were once woodland species but now live in cities. Birds such as pigeons also do well in cities because they are able to exploit urban food sources.

Island Ecosystems

Islands often have more different communities of plants and animals than the nearest mainland. The isolation of island habitats ensures that only certain species of plants and animals are able to reach and colonize them. Plant seeds are dispersed by wind and water, and flying animals such as birds, bats, and insects are common, but large, land-based predators are often absent. These conditions may cause island species to evolve along different lines than their mainland cousins. For example, many birds that have evolved on islands, such as New Zealand's kiwis, became flightless in the absence of predators. Island species are especially vulnerable to changes in their environment, whether these occur naturally or are caused by humans.

Animal Populations

In the wild, animal populations are held in balance by natural checks such as disease. In any particular year animal numbers may rise or fall, but they usually return to a consistent level over the course of several years. Competition for food among animals of the same species is one important factor. Different species within a community do not compete directly for food because they have different niches and eat slightly different foods.

A kiwi looks for food. These New Zealand birds are flightless and nocturnal (night active), searching out food at nighttime mainly by smell using their long, curved bills.

Predators and Prey

In any ecosystem predators curb numbers of herbivores (plant eaters), which in turn protects the plants at the base of the food chain. Many animal populations undergo a regular cycle of "boom and bust," which relates to factors such as climate. In years of harsh weather plant food is scarce, so herbivore and carnivore numbers stay low. In mild years plants thrive, and herbivores breed quickly. Increased numbers of prey prompt predators to multiply, but if they become too numerous, populations of their prey may crash. Then some predators starve, and their numbers drop, allowing herbivores to recover. In this way balance is restored.

Giraffes, zebras, and antelopes at a water hole in Namibia, Africa. These grazers and browsers eat slightly different plant foods, so they do not compete and can live in the same community.

THE HUMAN POPULATION EXPLOSION

In contrast to animal populations, which do not usually keep rising, the number of people on Earth has risen steeply in the last few centuries. Improved health care and more efficient farming practices mean that each year, more and more people live to an age at which they themselves can have children, so the human population "explodes." This huge increase puts great pressure on the natural resources on Earth and on ecosystems worldwide.

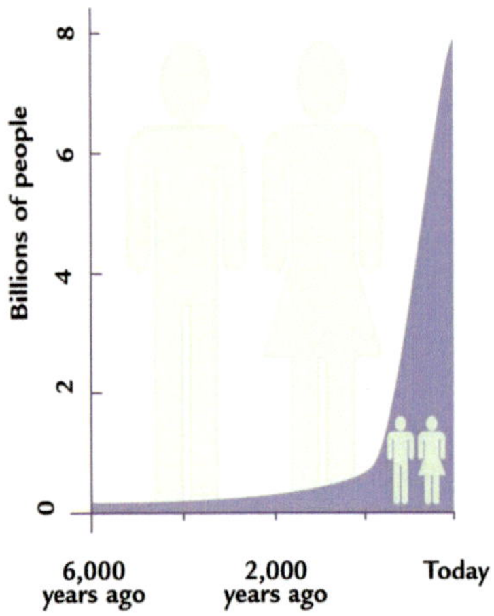

Some animals need larger territories to breed, feed, and shelter than others. Common murres are seabirds that need only very small territories like these nesting ledges (right) on which to lay their eggs.

Animal Territories

Many different types of animals, from fish to birds and mammals, establish group or individual territories. Each animal's "patch" contains enough food for the individual or group's needs, or is a safe place where the animals can breed or shelter. Animals defend their patch against others of their species, which limits the number of any one species a habitat will support. Animal territories thus help keep populations in balance.

Territory boundaries may be marked with scent or dung, or defined by audible calls or by visual shows of aggression. Animal territories vary greatly in size. For example, a pride of lions needs a huge territory in which to hunt, while seabirds such as common murres establish tiny territories on narrow cliff ledges just large enough for each bird to lay its eggs.

THE EFFECT OF HUMAN ANIMALS

In the 1800s the British economist Thomas Malthus (1766–1834) warned that human populations would expand very quickly unless checked by human-made or natural disasters such as war and disease. Charles Darwin, struck by Malthus's words, realized that animal and human populations were controlled by factors such as disease and competition. That helped him work out his famous theory of evolution by natural selection.

CHAPTER 5

Aquatic Ecosystems

Water covers 71 percent of the surface of Earth. Aquatic ecosystems range from freshwater systems, such as lakes, rivers, and wetlands, through saltwater systems, such as seas and oceans, to semisalty, or brackish, waters that are present in deltas, estuaries, and marshes.

Four main factors affect the nature of aquatic ecosystems. They are salinity (salt content), oxygen levels, the amount of sunlight that reaches the water, and water temperature. Salinity is measured in parts per thousand (ppt). Seawater contains 30 to 40 ppt, freshwater less than 1 ppt.

Sunlight penetrates only the upper waters of aquatic biomes. Moving waters such as swift-flowing streams and the surface of rough seas are particularly high in oxygen. The upper waters are also warmer than the depths, and water near the surface contains the most oxygen.

An aerial view of an oysterman's stilt house on the Mississippi delta. A delta is formed when the river splits into separate streams at the coast and dumps mud and particles to form new land.

UNDERWATER FOOD WEBS

Almost all life in aquatic habitats depends on the sun for energy, as on land. Aquatic food webs are as vast and complex as land-based webs. At the base of the food chain tiny plantlike, single-celled algae called phytoplankton floating at the surface harness the sun's energy through photosynthesis. In so doing, the phytoplankton produce a surprising 70 percent of the world's oxygen. Tiny animals called zooplankton feed on the phytoplankton and, in turn, provide food for larger creatures, and so on up the food chain. In the oceans small crustaceans called copepods and krill, part of the zooplankton, are food for the largest creatures, baleen whales. When aquatic organisms die, their remains are eaten either by scavengers such as shrimp and crabs or by microorganisms. The microorganisms break down organic remains into simpler compounds so their energy can be recycled.

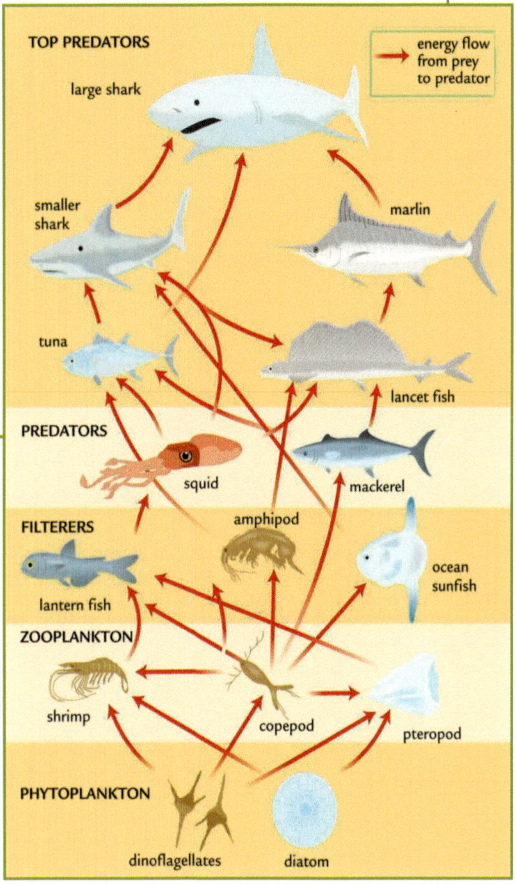

THE SALT IN SEAWATER

Seawater contains dissolved minerals from the land, which are washed into seas by rivers. The main minerals are sodium and chlorine in the form of salt (sodium chloride). Seawater also contains smaller amounts of other minerals, including calcium, potassium, and magnesium.

The Oceans

The oceans are by far the largest biome on Earth. They occupy two-thirds of the planet's surface and support an estimated 250,000 species of living organisms. Marine organisms can be divided into three groups, of which one is plankton—generally, small creatures and microorganisms that float on the water. The other groups are larger, actively swimming creatures, including fish,

THE FISH POPULATION

The oceans have always been a rich source of food for people and also for marine and shore predators. Since prehistoric times people of coastal regions worldwide have used nets, lines, and harpoons to harvest fish and other marine life.

In the last 100 years or so, fishing methods have become so efficient that fish populations have dropped steeply. Governments of fishing nations now set strict quotas to control the numbers of fish that can be caught, in an attempt to let fish stocks recover.

squid, and marine mammals; and smaller, less active creatures, including starfish, corals, sea anemones, sea lilies, and sponges that live on the bottom of the ocean.

Marine ecosystems can be divided into two main biomes: the open ocean, and the tidal zone—the shallow waters that edge the coasts. Tidal zone biomes include coral reefs, which are sometimes compared to rain forests because they support a huge diversity of life. In addition, there are shoreline ecosystems and semisalty habitats such as deltas and estuaries.

The deep, open ocean can be divided into vertical zones that can be compared to the vertical layers called stories that divide forest ecosystems. There are three main zones: the sunlit zone, the midwater, and the deep. Life is present at all depths of the ocean, but the sunlit upper waters are very productive and have the most biomass (amount of living material).

Life at the Surface

Plants and algae, including seaweeds, grow only in the sunlit upperwaters of the ocean or in coastal shallows on the seabed. In spring the phytoplankton multiply, or "bloom," in response to the longer hours of daylight, creating an abundance of food for herbivores (plant eaters). Some free-swimming creatures, including filter-feeding baleen whales, migrate long distances to feast on phytoplankton—or on herbivores.

Many fish of the upper waters, such as mackerel and herring, have dark backs and pale bellies. This coloration, termed countershading, helps conceal them both from seabirds hunting in the air above and from predators below. The seabirds cannot easily see the fish while looking toward the darkness of the water from above, nor can the ocean predators see the fish while looking toward the light from below.

Life for Bottom Dwellers

The ocean floor is as varied as the surface of the land, with features such as high ridges, tall peaks called seamounts, vast plains, and deep trenches. Bottoms may be rocky, sandy, or in the case of many deep oceans, covered with a layer of silty ooze. Plaice, rays, and other bottom-dwelling fish are adapted to their habitat with wide, flattened bodies for moving along the seabed. Some of these deep-sea creatures, such as sea spiders and the extraordinary tripod fish, have long legs or leglike spines that act as stilts and hold the animals high above the ooze.

Into the Depths

Food is scarce in the dark ocean depths. Fish and other deep-sea creatures feed on plant and animal remains that drift down from the waters above or prey on one another. Fish such as gulper eels and viperfish have huge jaws, sharp teeth, and stretchy stomachs so they can make the most of any prey they come across. Some deep-sea animals can swallow creatures twice their own size.

In the twilight zone, where dim light penetrates, some fish have rows of little lights on their bellies to disguise their shadow. The light may be produced either by special organs called photophores or by luminous (light-emitting) bacteria in the fish's skin.

In the deep oceans scientists discovered clams and tubeworms living

WATER ZONES UNDER THE OCEAN

The sunlit upper waters, called the euphotic zone, extend to a depth of 650 feet (195 m). Beyond that lies the midwater zone, which extends to about 6,500 feet (1,950 m). The upper waters of the midwater are sometimes called the twilight zone since some light reaches here, but no light penetrates below 3,000 feet (900 m) to the region called the dark zone. The deep-sea zone lies below 6,500 feet and may include ocean trenches descending to 35,000 feet (10,500 m). Each zone is home to a distinctive community of organisms; however, deep-diving creatures such as sperm whales regularly move between the zones.

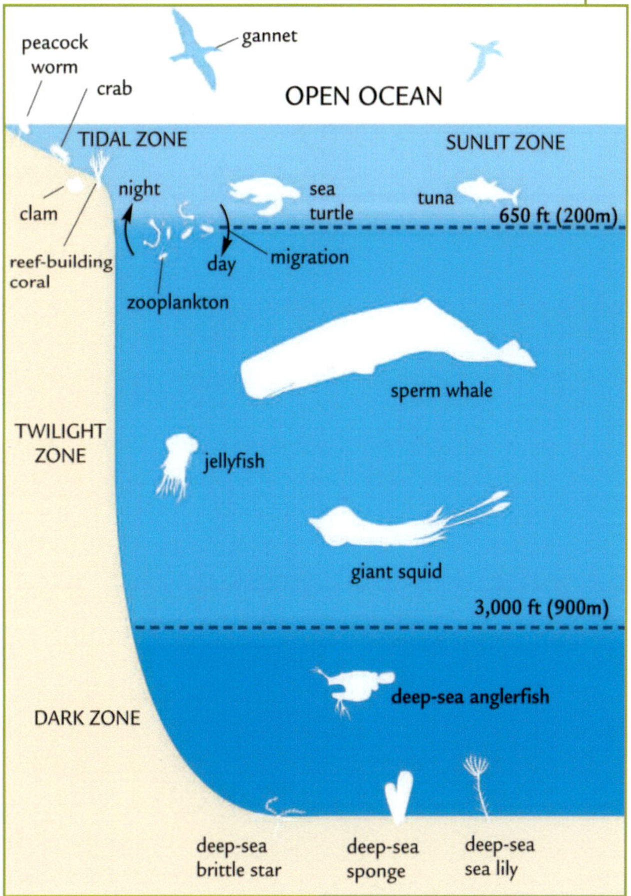

ARE THERE SEA MONSTERS?

In past times many people believed that huge, monstrous creatures lived in the ocean depths. One such creature was called the kraken, a legendary, many-armed beast that was said to rise from the depths to drag ships down to their doom. This legend is now thought to have been inspired by giant deep-sea squid. With the development of science, such superstitions faded. About 150 years ago scientists believed nothing could exist in the deep.

Now we know that monstrous-looking deep-sea fish do exist, but they are rarely more than 1 foot (30 cm) long.

A moray eel hides in a hole on the ocean floor. Moray eels live in warm seas and are predators that have sharp teeth.

EXPLORING THE DEPTHS

The ocean depths were one of the last places on Earth to be explored because of the great difficulties of deep undersea exploration. Submarines were developed in the 1870s, but they could not make deep dives. In 1934 U.S. naturalists Charles Beebe (1877-1962) and Otis Barton (1899-1992) descended to 2,500 feet (750 m) in a submarine called a bathysphere. In the 1960s Swiss naturalist Jacques Piccard (1922-2008) reached the deepest point in the oceans, the Mariana Trench in the Pacific, in a craft called a bathyscaphe. The Japanese bathyscaphe *Kaiko* explored the Mariana Trench in the 1990s. The U.S. Navy-owned deep submergence vehicle (DSV) *Alvin* has been used for ocean research since 1964. An eight-hour dive can take two scientists and a pilot to a depth of 14,764 feet (4,500 m).

TREASURES OF THE OCEAN

As well as seafood, the oceans yield many other useful products, including precious pearls and minerals such as manganese, which covers some parts of the seabed. The oceans also provide energy. For example, oil and natural gas can be mined from the seabed, and the power of waves and tides can be harnessed to produce electricity. Seawater can even provide fresh drinking water if the salt is removed through a process called desalination, but this is expensive.

around hydrothermal vents. These vents are cracks or chimneys from which black, billowing clouds of superhot, sulfur-rich water well up from inside Earth's crust.

The clams and worms do not depend on sunlight to make their food but get all their nutrients from bacteria inside their bodies. In turn, the bacteria get energy to make food from the sulfur present in the hydrothermal vents.

Exploring Coastal and Intertidal Zones

Tropical coral reefs are present in warm, clear, shallow-water areas. The reefs are made of the chalky skeletons of millions of small, sea anemonelike reef-building corals called coral polyps that build up on top of one another over thousands of years. Some coral reefs are 40–50 million years old and are made up of coral three-quarters of a mile (1.2 km) thick. The world's largest coral reef, Australia's Great Barrier Reef,

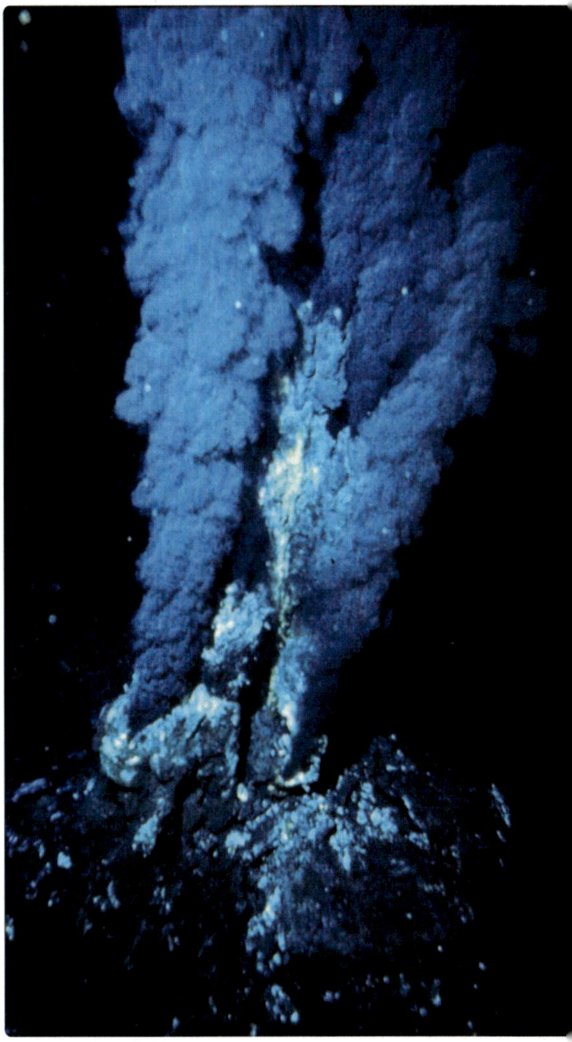

A vent called a black smoker on the midocean ridge, an undersea chain of mountains. The deep submergence vehicle (DSV) *Alvin* observed these in 1979.

PROTECTING THE REEFS

Coral reefs are the ocean's richest habitats, yet these amazing structures are now under threat throughout warm oceans. Pollution is one of the main dangers. Sewage from seaside towns and chemicals from farms and factories pollute the clear waters in which the polyps live. In some areas the coral is being mined to provide building materials or divers break off bits of reef as souvenirs. Global warming produces warmer seas, which is a massive danger causing coral animals to die and reefs to "bleach."

EXPLORING BEACH LIFE

Each pool on a beach is a mini-ecosystem. What can you find out about life in a pool on the nearest shore? First, is the beach sandy, rocky, or shingly? Is the pool situated on the upper, middle, or lower shore? Now analyze the pool itself. Is it deep? Do you think the water is very salty, or does it contain rainwater? Can you see any plants or seaweed? Now try to spot herbivores such as limpets and periwinkles, predators such as dog whelks, and scavengers such as shrimp and crabs. Can you draw a food web connecting the organisms you see?

stretches over 1,240 miles (2,000 km) and can be seen from space. In places it towers 500 feet (150 m) above the seabed. Coral reefs occupy only a small fraction of coastal waters worldwide, but these ecosystems support an estimated 25 percent of marine life, providing food, shelter, and hundreds of hiding places for many creatures. One of the reefs at Key Largo, in Florida, has more than 550 species.

Life on Seashores

Worldwide, there are more than 350,000 miles (560,000 km) of coastline. Rocky, shingly, sandy, and muddy beaches each host their own communities of life. Rocky shores are rich in wildlife, including seaweeds, barnacles, shrimps, limpets, sea anemones, and crabs. Cockles, clams, and razor shells live on sandy beaches. Many sandy-beach animals burrow for protection from predators and so as not to dry out when the tide is out.

Seashores are harsh habitats, where conditions are continuously changing. The animals and plants

ZONES OF THE SEASHORE

Seashores are divided into three zones between the high- and low-tide mark: the upper, middle, and lower shore. Each is home to distinctive plants, animals, and other life. Beyond the upper zone lies the splash zone, where rocks are misted by salt spray and stained with lichen. Limpets, periwinkles, barnacles, shrimp, and wrack seaweeds are present on the upper and middle shore. Lobsters, sea anemones, sea urchins, kelp, and fish such as lumpfish thrive in pools on the lower shore.

living there spend part of each day covered by water and the remainder exposed to the weather, which may be baking sunshine, winds, or rain. Organisms have to adapt to these two different lifestyles. They time their resting and feeding periods to match the rhythm of the tides.

POLLUTION AND OXYGEN LEVELS

The levels of oxygen in freshwater habitats are affected by pollution, which can harm local wildlife. Fertilizers used in farming contain nutrients. Water drained from fields makes freshwater systems superrich in nutrients, which causes algae and bacteria to multiply. Algae blanket the water surface and block sunlight from plants that produce oxygen. As algae die, oxygen-consuming microorganisms eat the algae and use up lots of oxygen. As a result, fish and other wildlife suffocate.

Freshwater Ecosystems

Freshwater covers only a small part of Earth's surface but offers a range of habitats. Freshwater ecosystems may be divided into still-water systems, such as lakes, ponds, swamps, and marshes, and habitats with flowing water, namely, rivers and streams. As in the oceans, the productivity of freshwater habitats is affected by many factors. These factors include soil type, water depth, water temperature, sunlight and oxygen levels, minerals, and pollution. Freshwater habitats rich in nutrients and organic matter are also rich in life. Wetlands fed by water from acidic rocks or peaty ground are low in nutrients.

PRODUCTS OF WETLANDS

Rivers, lakes, and other bodies of freshwater have countless uses. Most important, they supply water for wildlife and also for human settlements, farming, and industry. Around the world many settlements are located by rivers, lakes, and other wetlands or on the coast. Wetlands act as reservoirs and also help prevent flooding after heavy rain has fallen by soaking up excess water. They also provide a wealth of food from fish, shellfish, and waterfowl to fruit and crops such as rice. Aquatic mammals such as otters and muskrats once yielded valuable fur for clothing. Timber and materials like rushes, traditionally used in roofing (right), also come from wetlands.

MAKING YOUR OWN MINI-POND

Build a mini-pond in your backyard using an old washbowl or a piece of plastic sheeting. First, ask adults for their help to choose a good site for the pond. Dig a bowl-shaped hollow with a spade or trowel, place the bowl or plastic sheeting inside, then firm the soil back around the edge. Cover the bottom with a layer of gravel, then put stones around the edge and on the bottom. Add water plants, and fill the pond with water. It won't be long until wildlife begins to colonize (move into) the pond.

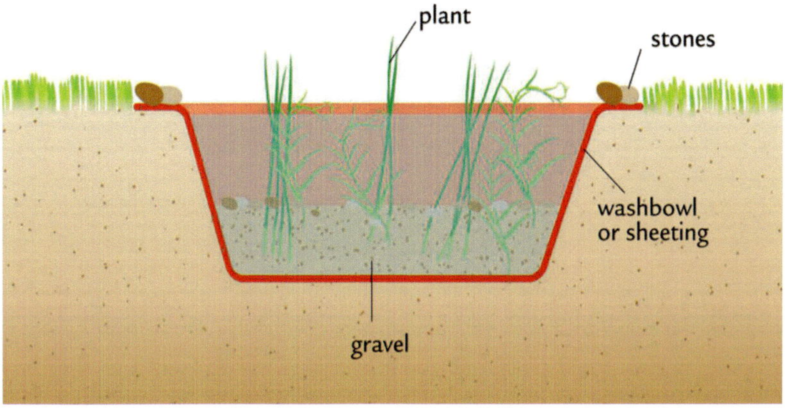

CHAPTER 6

The Human Impact on Earth

The human population is ever-increasing, a factor that puts enormous pressure on the natural world. Human activity threatens to destroy many of Earth's valuable ecosystems.

A rolling field of wheat in Spokane County, Washington. Farmers in the United States use crop rotation and fertilizers in order to avoid exhausting soil nutrients. Next year, this same field might contain soybeans or another crop.

Modern human civilization began over 10,000 years ago as people began to grow crops in parts of the Middle East and, somewhat later, Egypt, northern India, and China. Settlements grew up in places where people could find food and water, and also safety from their enemies. Farmers learned to irrigate the land so that crops could be grown. New techniques and machinery gradually made farming ever more efficient. Now many modern crop fields are "green deserts" where just one plant, the crop, is nurtured at the expense of wild plants and insect life, which farmers poison with pesticides and herbicides.

From the 1790s the Industrial Revolution saw the start of modern manufacturing methods. Now factories are built all over the world and modern industries use up huge amounts of energy and natural resources, and produce considerable amounts of pollution in the process.

EARLY SETTLEMENTS

More than 8,000 years ago one of the world's oldest towns, Çatal Höyük, existed in what is now Turkey. It grew up near a range of hills where a hard volcanic stone called obsidian was mined. This was used to make tools and weapons, and was also traded. Many of the world's first settlements sprang up to exploit natural resources like this. In the Middle East, Egypt, India, and China the first major cities were built on the banks of rivers that provided transportation, water, and protection against enemy attacks.

THE GROWTH OF CITIES

Many cities that were founded just a few centuries ago are now huge and prosperous. The world's biggest cities include Mexico City, Sao Paolo, Seoul, Tokyo, Moscow, London, and New York.

In overcrowded cities hygiene, sewage management, and even available clean water may be a problem, particularly in developing countries. More than half the world's population now lives in cities.

In the last 20 years the human population has mushroomed. In 1980 there were about 4 billion people on Earth; by 2020 this was 7.8 billion. Experts think there may be 9 billion by 2050. This puts a huge strain on natural resources and the environment.

Habitat Destruction

One of the main effects of the growing number of people on Earth is habitat destruction, as people take over the natural habitats where wild species once lived. Every year more and more wild land is plowed just to grow enough food for people or to graze domestic livestock. Overgrazed land is prone to erosion; the animals eat or trample everything, including the roots that hold together the soil.

A green turtle covers her eggs in the sand. Care must be taken to stop tourists from disrupting such important wildlife activities.

A DANGER TO WETLANDS

Around the world natural wetlands are disappearing fast. They are being drained to provide land for farming or new sites for factories and towns. Rivers and other freshwater systems are mined for gold and gemstones, building materials such as sand and gravel, or fuels such as peat. Some wetlands also disappear as they dry or silt up naturally, or when the land subsides. The United States has lost half its wetlands since the start of European settlement. Two-thirds of Europe's wetlands have completely vanished in the last 300 years.

DESTRUCTION OF THE RAIN FOREST

Tropical rain forests contain the greatest biodiversity of any habitat on Earth. Experts estimate that around two-thirds of all species live there. However, this precious habitat is also disappearing faster than any other. Tropical rain forests now occupy less than half the area they did just a century ago. These forests are being felled for their valuable hardwood timber (below) or for fuel and to clear land to grow crops and ranch cattle. Mining and dam building are also nibbling away at forests in some areas. This problem is called deforestation.

Destruction of the rain forests harms the balance of gases in the atmosphere and affects the world's climate. Forest trees absorb a large amount of carbon dioxide and so increase oxygen levels in the atmosphere. Felled trees can no longer take in carbon dioxide or release oxygen.

In addition, when the forests are burned to clear the land, carbon is released, which adds to the levels of carbon dioxide in the atmosphere. Since carbon dioxide is a greenhouse gas, deforestation contributes to the problem of global warming—rising temperatures worldwide.

HUNTED TO EXTINCTION

The thylacine was sometimes called the "Tasmanian wolf" from its dog-like appearance, or the "Tasmanian tiger" due to its stripes. However, it was neither. It was a marsupial (pouched mammal), related to kangaroos and koalas. From the 1800s European settlers hunted thylacines because they killed their livestock. Wiped out on the Australian mainland, the last individual died in Hobart Zoo, Tasmania, in 1936.

Huge areas of land also disappear under concrete as new towns and industrial parks spring up, and roads, railroads, and powerlines are blazed through forests, deserts, and wildernesses. In many parts of the world governments have handed over wild land to mining companies to dig or drill for minerals and fuel, or to construction firms to build dams to produce hydroelectric power. The tourist industry also puts increasing pressure on wild areas such as mountain regions, coral reefs, and sandy beaches. Many people like to "get back to nature" on vacation, yet sprawling resorts can spoil the scenery that tourists come to enjoy. Large numbers of visitors can disturb wildlife such as turtles nesting on beaches.

The Effects of Hunting

Overexploitation of the world's wildlife has become a major problem as human numbers have risen. For thousands of years people have hunted animals on land and in rivers and oceans for meat and also for hides, fur, or feathers. When the human population was smaller, this hunting did little harm. In recent centuries the invention of guns, explosive harpoons, and devices such as

WHALING AND THE WHALE POPULATION

The European whaling industry began around 1600. In the 1700s, 1800s, and early 1900s whales were hunted relentlessly for their meat, oil, bones, and baleen (hornlike material on the upper jaw). By 1950 many of the once-numerous great whales were almost extinct. In the 1990s some whaling was banned by many nations. Now that the mass slaughter has ended, many whale populations have begun to recover.

sonar used to detect fish, have made the killing of animals much easier. Overhunting and overfishing now threaten the survival of many ocean and land species. In addition to hunting for food, dangerous animals such as tigers, sharks, and snakes are often hunted because people fear them as killers. Elephants, rhinoceroses, and big cats are killed, often illegally, for their ivory or fur. Elsewhere animals as diverse as monkeys, parrots, and terrapins are threatened by the pet trade. Animals captured in the wild rarely survive long in captivity. In the past, overhunting killed off species such as the dodo. Ecologists predict that thousands more species may soon go the same way.

Introducing a Species

Every ecosystem on Earth has its own community of plants, animals, and other

CANE TOAD OVERPOPULATION

In the 1930s a panel of experts recommended that the cane toad of Central America should be introduced to Australia to control beetle pests in the sugar cane plantations there. These amphibians were duly taken to Australia and released. Unfortunately, the large, poisonous toads bred quickly and are now a huge threat to native frogs, reptiles, birds and even small mammals.

organisms that are specifically suited to their particular environment. The introduction of new species to an area can upset the natural balance of life. All over the world people have introduced nonnative plants and animals to provide food, to control native species seen as pests, or simply to improve the scenery. If the new arrivals thrive and multiply, they quickly crowd out and threaten the original native species there.

The Effects of Pollution

Pollution means any form of contamination of land, air, or water and is mostly caused by people. It may be deliberate or happen accidentally. Pollution is spread through the air by winds, by currents in moving water, and through the soil by seeping groundwater. Once in the ecosystem the contamination is absorbed by wildlife at a point in the food chain and passes up through the chain as carnivores eat herbivores. Top predators that feed on large numbers of polluted prey are sometimes the most contaminated of all. In the early 1960s, for example, the American bald eagle nearly died out because pesticide concentrations built up in its prey and thus within the eagles' own bodies. As a result, their eggshells became too fragile for the eggs to survive.

Smog caused by burning coal pollutes the air over Beijing, China. Burning fossil fuels like coal and oil releases poisonous vapors into the atmosphere.

Human activities such as mining, manufacturing, energy production, and farming produce substantial amounts of pollution. So does the waste we produce daily in our homes, offices, and schools. Fossil fuels (oil, gas, and coal) burned in factories, power plants, and cars release toxic fumes into the atmosphere. Car exhausts spew out carbon dioxide, carbon monoxide, and tiny particles. Devices called catalytic converters have reduced this pollution, but these poisonous gases are a major cause of the dirty smog that hangs in the air over major cities, causing breathing problems.

Rivers, lakes, and oceans are polluted by chemicals from factories and by fertilizers and pesticides used in farming. The soil

CHERNOBYL

In 1986 one of the world's worst-ever pollution disasters was caused by an accident at a nuclear power plant. The nuclear reactor at Chernobyl in northern Ukraine (below) caught fire and exploded. A cloud of radioactive gas escaped and was spread over a vast area by the wind. It contaminated tundra vegetation in Siberia and Scandinavia, which poisoned wildlife such as reindeer. Thousands of deer had to be destroyed.

A LOOK AT WATER POLLUTION

The presence of certain aquatic creatures in streams and rivers gives clues about the water quality. Caddisfly and mayfly larvae and freshwater shrimp thrive only in water that is clean. See if these creatures can be found in a stream or pond near you. Take care not to get too close to the edge and fall in. Use a net to sweep the water, then transfer your catch to a bowl while you identify the species using a field guide. Return the mini-beasts to the water after you have finished looking at them.

POLAR REGION POLLUTION

Although the polar regions are generally far away from major towns and industrial centers that release pollution, these regions are rich in minerals that can cause contamination of both the land and the sea. In the Arctic, mining and drilling for gold, uranium, lead, coal, oil, and natural gas have caused considerable pollution on land and in the water. The Antarctic is also rich in minerals, but the continent is a wildlife sanctuary, so no mining is allowed there. However, traces of pollution from distant sources, such as radioactive contamination from Chernobyl, have been found in the Antarctic ice.

is poisoned by chemicals from industry, mining, and agriculture, and also by the disposal of waste in sites called landfills. The problem of how to deal with all the waste we produce in our homes and factories becomes bigger each year.

Pollution in the Oceans

Over the centuries oceans have been used as a dumping ground for sewage and all types of dangerous chemicals. Today a staggering 20 million tons of rubbish are dumped in the oceans every year, including huge items of junk such as discarded oil rigs. Coastal waters are often the most heavily polluted areas because pipes discharge raw sewage and chemicals into the shallows. Filter feeders and scavengers such as mollusks and crustaceans absorb the pollution and are then eaten by fish and other predators. Researchers in the Arctic have monitored pollution levels in top predators such as polar bears that feed on fish and seals. Some bears contained so much poison they could be classed as toxic waste.

WHAT IS ACID RAIN?

Acid rain is a form of pollution that results when nitrogen oxide from car exhausts and sulfur dioxide from power plants enter the atmosphere. These gases mix with water vapor in the air to form weak acids, which then fall as rain. Acid rain can kill trees, harm wildlife, and eat away at buildings (below).

An oil-coated sea bird struggles on the rocks at the north shore of Seal Island on Alaska's Prince William Sound after hundreds of tons of oil were spilled into the sea from a tanker in 1989.

Hazards Caused by Pollution

Pollution of the air, water, and land has led to a number of serious environmental problems. One of them is global warming, caused by the increase in greenhouse gases in the atmosphere partly due to burning fossil fuels. The warmer weather causes ice in the polar regions to melt. If this continues, rising sea levels may threaten low-lying coastal regions, such as Louisiana, Bangladesh, and the Netherlands. Ozone loss in the atmosphere, formerly caused by polluting CFC chemicals, has meant more harmful UV radiation reaching Earth.

The Effects of Oil Spills

Oil spills are a major source of marine pollution. One of the worst-ever oil spills

IMPACT OF GREENHOUSE GASES

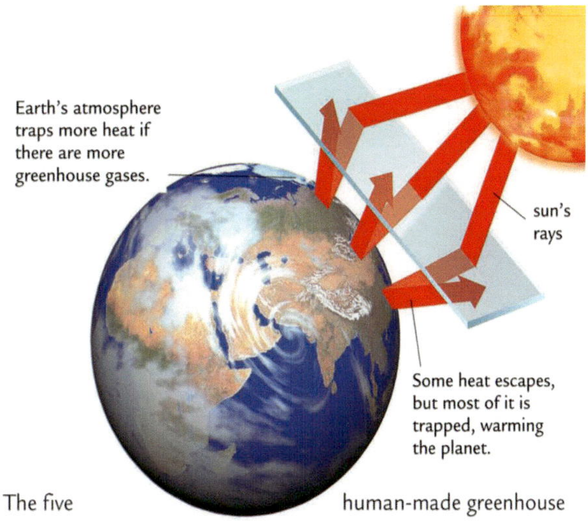

The five natural greenhouse gases are water vapor, carbon dioxide, methane, nitrous oxide, and ozone. The atmosphere also contains human-made greenhouse gases called chlorofluorocarbons (CFCs). As the level of greenhouse gases increases, Earth's climate changes—an effect called global warming.

CARSON'S SILENT SPRING

In the 1960s pioneering U.S. ecologist Rachel Carson (1907–1964) warned of the dangers of a pesticide called DDT, which poisoned wildlife. In her book *Silent Spring* she predicted that the use of chemicals such as DDT in agriculture would eventually lead to a world that was barren of wildlife, where no birds would sing. Carson's campaign eventually succeeded, and DDT was banned worldwide, apart from specialized uses, in 2004.

affected a huge area of Arctic coast.
In 1989 the Exxon oil tanker *Valdez* ran aground off Prince William Sound in Alaska, spilling 50,000 tons of oil into the sea. More than 1,200 miles (1,900 km) of coastline were polluted, and thousands of birds, sea otters, fish, and shellfish died. The disaster cost billions of dollars to clean up.

Changing Human Impact

What can be done to reduce pollution and other damage to the natural world? The effects of habitat destruction can be reduced by creating sanctuaries and reserves where no development is allowed. Building on

Workers harvest zucchini on an organic farm. Organic farmers do not use artificial fertilizers and pesticides, and so reduce the harmful effect of agriculture on the environment.

ECOTOURISM

In many parts of the world ecotourism now helps to protect wildlife. Ecotourists are people who pay to see wildlife in natural surroundings such as reserves. Their money helps to pay for the park upkeep and for local conservation programs. Ecotourism has helped conservation work in reserves worldwide, such as Australia's Great Barrier Reef, Antarctica, and in Nepal's Annapurna mountain sanctuary.

brown field sites—empty ground in city centers—instead of in the surrounding countryside can preserve wild habitats on the edge of towns. Replanting can restore lost forests, and careful management of land can prevent erosion. Organic farming, in which farmers avoid chemical fertilizers and pesticides and rely on traditional methods such as crop rotation, can minimize the impact of farming on the environment. The major cause of pollution and habitat destruction is the human population explosion, which can be curbed by more effective birth control.

Governments around the world are introducing laws to control the release of chemicals by cities, industry, and agriculture. Cooperation is needed to tackle ozone loss and global warming. In 1987 all nations agreed not to use CFCs, which cause ozone loss. Governments have agreed on targets to reduce greenhouse gas emissions. Renewable energy sources such as solar, wind, and water power can slow down global warming and people can tackle pollution by using less energy and chemicals and reducing waste.

ENERGY CONSERVATION AND RECYCLING

We can all tackle the problems of global warming and acid rain by saving energy and recycling household waste.

Think about ways in which your family or school could save energy. Switching off lights and machines when they are not needed, turning down the central heating, and making compost from vegetable peelings can help. So can using the car less. Note down all the car journeys your family makes in a week. Are they all necessary, or could you walk, cycle, or take public transportation instead? Taking old cans, bottles, paper, and plastic packaging to recycling centers so they can be used again reduces waste, and ask people to use less water and fewer chemicals and fertilizers on lawns.

CHAPTER 7

Conservation Programs

Conservation is the action taken by people to protect and preserve the natural world and its resources. In particular, conservation scientists aim to prevent the extinction of living things and preserve their unique habitats.

Generally, people agree that natural resources should not be used up or wasted, but they may have different views about what makes a good conservation plan for a particular region. People often disagree about the right balance between environmental interests and economic ones. Sometimes scientists think that a habitat should be preserved and protected but differ on how people should use the area. For example, someone who visits a national park to relax

← Children looking at a tidal rock pool. Many different types of living organisms inhabit such an ecosystem. It is important to carefully preserve these types of natural resources.

↑ Tourists check out a leopard as it crosses the track in the Kruger National Park, South Africa. National parks help to prevent poaching of wildlife by hunters.

or enjoy listening to animal sounds does not appreciate someone else who uses a snowmobile or motorized all-terrain vehicle in the same area. People who participate in bird watching or hiking activities do not want to do so at the same time that others are hunting wild game. A major role of conservation biologists is to settle such conflicts.

Principles of Conservation

People who try to preserve the natural world (conservationists) believe it is very important to look after the land and water as well as living organisms. Sometimes the best conservation plan to protect a habitat is to limit the number of people allowed in and let the ecosystem operate naturally. Conservation biologists consider three basic principles for developing a conservation plan. First, that evolutionary change is a basic process in any living system. All species in natural ecosystems respond

THE AMERICAN BISON

Millions of American bison once roamed freely across the open plains of North America. Many Native American peoples depended on them for food, clothing, and shelter.

In 1830 the U.S. government began killing the bison to control the Native Americans. By 1900 fewer than 1,000 bison were left, and conservationists worked hard to save them.

A beaver building a dam can affect other species nearby.

to environmental change, so conservation plans must consider how species can respond based on their history. Long-term conservation plans that involve changing and managing habitats need to consider differences in the life styles of various living organisms as a consequence of their evolutionary past. Many insects, small mammals, and native grasses live no longer than a year, while freshwater turtles, tortoises, and oak trees grow for several

ORIGINS OF CONSERVATION

Several centuries after the colonization of North America by Europeans, people began to realize that natural resources were limited and could be used up by activities such as clearing forests and building towns, cities, and factories.

In the 19th century the writer Henry David Thoreau (1817–1862) promoted an idea called the romantic-transcendental conservation ethic (an harmonious appreciation of and coexistence with nature). During the same century the naturalist John Muir (1838–1914) helped to set up the Sierra Club, which encouraged people to enjoy, learn about, and preserve natural settings. His efforts contributed to the creation of several national parks, including Yosemite.

The resource conservation ethic, promoted by forester Gifford Pinchot (1865–1946), was based directly on economics and commercial interests. Pinchot believed that natural resources, including forests, should be used to produce materials for human use. This viewpoint led to a type of forest management in which commercial markets were built into the conservation plan so that timber production, mining, hunting, and fishing were balanced against habitat and wildlife preservation.

The most scientific approach to conservation, the evolutionary-ecological land ethic, was developed by the naturalist Aldo Leopold (1887–1948) in the early 20th century. Leopold viewed natural ecosystems as being complex, interworking parts. Most scientists engaged in conservation programs today support many of these views.

Modern approaches to conservation work combine the three ethics identified.

years before becoming adults, maturing and then producing offspring. The second principle is that the environment is always changing because of factors such as weather, season, and species interactions. Modern conservation biologists do not expect the pattern of distribution and the number of plant and animal species in an area to remain the same. This principle goes against an earlier concept that nature is in a balanced state. Conservation plans should be based on an understanding that the types of species and population levels always change. For example, if beavers move into an area with a small stream, they usually build dams that

LOVELOCK'S GAIA HYPOTHESIS

In the 1960s British scientist James Lovelock (born 1919) published what he called the Gaia hypothesis. It is the idea that Earth's oceans, atmosphere, and land-masses are held in equilibrium (balance) by all the living organisms of the planet, including humans. The hypothesis is that the living world operates like a superorganism, keeping a worldwide environmental balance. However, not all scientists agree with Lovelock's idea.

Inuit whalers landing a bowhead whale. Conservation plans are built around the Inuits' whale-hunting customs.

Setting aside areas as national parks, such as Yellowstone National Park, helps protect living organisms.

make ponds that might attract some species, such as wading birds. Decreasing the stream flow might result in there being a reduction in certain other species, such as streamside salamanders.

The third and final principle of any conservation plan is human society. Human needs and preferences can easily cause conflict and disagreement. There are situations in which conservation biologists must think about the needs or desires of the original inhabitants of a region. For example, conservation plans to preserve and protect natural habitats

ROADS AND ANIMAL POPULATIONS

Loss of habitat is one of the greatest threats to animals in most countries, and highways are a major cause. In the United States highways take up around 1 percent of the land surface, and several million animals are killed on the roads every day. By noting the number of road-killed animals in an area, particularly after a highway has been newly built, conservationists can find out how badly natural habitats are affected and help make people aware of the importance of finding ways to prevent as many animals as possible from being killed in this way.

Signboards provide information for visitors to Penguin Island Conservation Park, home to Western Australia's largest population of little penguins. Many countries establish parks to help preserve wildlife and habitats.

in Australia now include the attitudes and feelings of the aboriginal peoples, who are the original Australian inhabitants. Similarly, the International Whaling Commission (IWC) has a quota (allowance) for the hunting of bowhead whales. This permits Alaskan Inuits and the native people of Chukotka, Russia, to follow their cultural traditions of whale hunting.

Benefits of Ecological Reserves

One of the greatest threats to biodiversity and ecosystems is the destruction of habitats. Conservation programs have resulted in the establishment of ecological reserves that protect species from human activities and allow them to live in these regions. Many countries have put aside land, freshwater, seashore, and marine habitats as national parks and wildlife refuges for the protection of living organisms.

One of the most successful conservation approaches ever taken in the United States was the setting aside of natural lands as national parks. Yellowstone National Park in the western United States, established by Congress in 1872, was the world's first national park. Royal National Park near Sydney, Australia, established in 1879,

YOUR OWN BACKYARD

A basic principle of conservation programs is that more natural habitats mean more native wildlife. Large ecological reserves are often part of regional conservation plans, but you can see the positive effects by creating a habitat on a much smaller scale, such as in your backyard. You need four basic things to develop and maintain a backyard habitat—food, water, shelter, and places for animals to have young. You also need a mix of shrubbery, trees, and open areas to make an ecologically diverse habitat that reinforces the importance of creating ecological reserves.

became the second. Many countries in Africa, Europe, Asia, and tropical America have also used the national park concept of conservation, and hundreds of protected habitats now exist around the world.

Marine Conservation

Conservation programs for marine mammals are important worldwide and often involve international politics. The International Whaling Commission was established in 1946 to protect whale species from overhunting and achieve the best population levels of commercial species. In this way whale hunting could carry on without all the whales being killed. However, Norway and Japan, countries that have always hunted whales, have exceeded IWC quotas, and in 2019 Japan left the IWC.

Breeding in Captivity

When an animal species is threatened by extinction, conservationists may collect some of the animals and breed them in captivity. Many captive-breeding programs have been successful, including those with the peregrine falcon. In the 1950s and 1960s many farmers used pesticides to improve their crop yields, but the chemicals built up in wildlife in the food web. Because the falcons fed on contaminated prey, the eggshells of many birds become fragile.

A peregrine falcon acts as foster parent to captive-bred foster chicks. The 1972 ban on pesticides that had affected falcon eggs, in addition to captive breeding, has increased their population numbers.

HELPING MARINE TURTLES

Marine turtles are at risk of becoming extinct. There are several causes for this, including disruption of their breeding by human interference. Some people have collected and eaten the turtle eggs they find near beaches; others have made turtle soup from adult green turtles. In Australia red foxes have preyed on turtle nests. Even though there are laws to protect the marine turtles, their population levels are still very low. In some places turtle eggs are taken indoors until they hatch, then the young turtles are released. Do you think this will solve the problem of marine turtles becoming extinct?

Young peregrine falcons failed to hatch and numbers declined. In 1960 no breeding pairs were known to exist in the eastern United States. Ten years later a captive-breeding program was started with peregrines from the western United States and Europe. It was a success and in 1974 the first peregrine falcons were released back into the wild. Now the falcons breed successfully in many of the places in which they once lived.

Settlers and Explorers

Without conservation plans to prevent the exploitation and destruction of natural resources even small numbers of humans can wipe out species simply by moving into their habitats and outcompeting them.

Some conservation biologists think that explorers and settlers throughout the world have wiped out countless species that were easily preyed on by people. The Polynesian

THE IMPACT OF CAPTIVE BREEDING

Although some endangered species protected in zoos and other facilities have been bred successfully, then released back into the wild, some serious problems with the programs have emerged. Any excessive hunting, pollution, or habitat destruction that put the species in danger in the first place still exists in most cases. Therefore it turns out that simply adding more animals into an already troubled habitat is not as effective a conservation measure as it might be.

settlers called Maoris, for example, killed off a group of flightless birds called moas in New Zealand. These birds were among the largest ever known, some standing more than 10 feet (3 m) tall. They were not scared of humans and were not adapted to escape from hunters; they had no defenses against the settlers and could not fly away from danger. Most species of moas were extinct within 100 years of the settlers' arrival.

Protecting Pandas

Scientists monitored the effectiveness of setting aside habitats in order to protect wildlife from human activities at a large ecological reserve for giant pandas in China. Surprisingly they found that the panda habitat had declined in quality and decreased in size since the reserve had been established in 1975. A rapid increase in the human population within the reserve, which led to increased tourism, removal of wood, and new road construction, was considered to be the main cause of the ecological degradation and habitat loss.

The results of this conservation survey reinforced the principle that effective wildlife conservation plans must always include consideration of human factors, activities, and needs.

A giant panda and her cub feed on bamboo shoots. Habitat loss is a major reason for decline in panda numbers, but since the 2000s these are slowly recovering.

CHAPTER 8

BIOGRAPHY

Alexander von Humboldt

In the late 1700s scientists began to reassess their views of the natural world, and to turn to direct observation, careful measurement and experimentation. Exploration went hand in hand with scientific discovery, and Alexander von Humboldt, who traveled widely in Europe and South America, became a pioneer in the field of botany.

The naturalist and explorer Alexander von Humboldt was, at the height of his career, one of the most famous people in Europe. His full name was Friedrich Wilhelm Heinrich Alexander, Baron von Humboldt, and he was born in Berlin on September 14, 1769, into a family closely involved with the political and intellectual life of the city. Berlin was the capital of Prussia, the most important of the independent states that would later be united as the country of Germany. It was ruled by Frederick II, known as Frederick the Great (1712–1786), who was a leading figure in Europe.

Humboldt studied at the University of Göttingen for a year, where he became interested in natural science, particularly in

← Alexander von Humboldt, shown here in a portrait from 1806, is credited with the foundation of the field of biogeography.

KEY DATES

1769	Born September 14, in Berlin
1779	Education begins with private tutors
1789	Enrolls as a student at the University of Göttingen
1790	Sets off on tour of Europe with Georg Forster
1791	Enters the Freiberg School of Mining
1792–97	Visits salt-mining regions of central Europe
1793	Is appointed assessor, then director, of mines in Bayreuth
1796	Humboldt's mother dies
1797	Publishes results of experiments on the effect of electricity on muscles
1799	Sails for South America with Aimé Bonpland
1800	In February Humboldt and Bonpland head inland from Caracas to find the headwaters of the Orinoco, they discover the Casiquiare canal; in November they sail to Cuba
1801	Humboldt and Bonpland return to Colombia in March; set off to cross the Andes
1802	Humboldt and Bonpland climb Mount Chimborazo; on November 8 Humboldt observes transit of Mercury, when the planet crosses the disk of the Sun
1803	In February Humboldt sails for Mexico
1804	On June 30 sails for Europe; on return meets Simón Bolívar
1805	Visits Italy to study Mount Vesuvius with Joseph Gay-Lussac and Christian Leopold von Buch; publishes *Essay on the Geography of Plants*
1805–34	Publishes *Personal Narrative*
1807	Sent to Paris as a member of the Prussian delegation; publishes *Views of Nature*
1808	Settles in Paris
1826	Publishes *Political Essay on the Island of Cuba*
1827	Returns to Berlin
1828	Becomes a founding member of the Geographic Society; opens a Berlin meeting of the Society of Natural Scientists and Physicians
1829	Visits Russia
1845–62	*Cosmos* published in five volumes
1859	Dies on May 6, in Berlin

mineralogy (the study of minerals, such as gold, iron, and coal, and of mining), and in geology (the study of the history, structure, and composition of Earth). These were among the very latest subjects to be taught in universities, and would soon prove important as European countries sought to develop industrially (using coal and iron in particular) in the early 19th century.

While he was at the university Humboldt met the naturalist Georg Forster (1754–1794), who had sailed with the English navigator Captain James Cook (1728–1779) on his second voyage around the world. Hearing of Forster's scientific explorations in the Pacific may well have inspired Humboldt's later decision to undertake his own journey to South America. In the meantime Forster and Humboldt planned a grand tour of Europe. They set off in 1790 along the River Rhine and through the Netherlands, and from there undertook the short sea crossing to England.

Alexander von Humboldt travels through and explores the mountain ranges of South America near Cajambe volcano in this painting by Gianni Dagli Orti.

SCIENTIFIC VOYAGES

The first voyages of discovery by Europeans had taken place in the 15th century. In the early years these great voyages were undertaken by individuals who saw them as a chance to gain riches through trading and mineral finds, and to earn the gratitude of their monarchs by claiming lands for their country. In the 17th century scientific curiosity became an additional motivating factor, and by the 18th and 19th centuries governments actually sponsored such voyages.

Captain Cook's First Voyage

In 1768 the ship the *Endeavour* set sail from England under the captaincy of the Englishman James Cook. The voyage was organized by the Royal Society and the British Admiralty in London, and its declared purpose was the observation of the passage of Venus across the sun—known as the transit of Venus—from the southern hemisphere. It was hoped this would help astronomers to work out Earth's distance from the sun. The voyage was also a chance for wider scientific exploration, so on board *Endeavour* was the English naturalist Joseph Banks (1743-1820); the ship had "a fine library of Natural History."

After observing the transit of Venus from Tahiti in the Pacific, Cook traveled around New Zealand. In 1770 he reached Australia, the east coast of which he surveyed, mapped, and claimed for Britain. Banks was able to indulge his passion for botany, gathering vast quantities of plant specimens and recording what he saw; the natural life there was so abundant that Cook named the area—south of what is now Sydney—Botany Bay.

Cook took the German naturalists Johann and Georg Forster on his second voyage of discovery to the Pacific and Antarctica. This painting shows Cook's arrival on the Pacific islands of the New Hebrides in 1774.

Neptunism and Plutonism

Humboldt returned to Prussia having developed a keen interest in science, but also with the realization that he would need a proper scientific education. In 1791 he entered the Freiberg School of Mining and graduated after two years.

The head of the School of Mining at this time was Abraham Gottlob Werner (1749–1817). Werner was the originator of the theory of Neptunism—named for Neptune, Roman god of the sea—which maintained that an ocean once covered the entire world, as described in the biblical story of Noah's flood. Werner believed that, as the water receded, all the minerals were precipitated out of it to form layers (strata) of sedimentary rocks, which were laid down in a precise order. Werner also held that volcanoes were of more recent origin, caused by the burning of underground coal beds. Set against this theory was the one put forward by Scottish geologist James Hutton (1726–1797), who thought that Earth must have been formed over millions of years, and that it was still going through the process. Hutton believed that heat from the center of Earth caused rock formations, most obviously through volcanic action. Since volcanoes were associated in ancient times with Pluto, the god of the underworld, Hutton's theory became known as Plutonism. As a student of Werner, Humboldt originally accepted Werner's Neptunist views, but what he saw on his later travels eventually converted him to Plutonism.

Alexander von Humboldt painted in 1843. He holds his manuscript for *Cosmos: A Sketch of a Physical Description of the Universe*, which was published after his death.

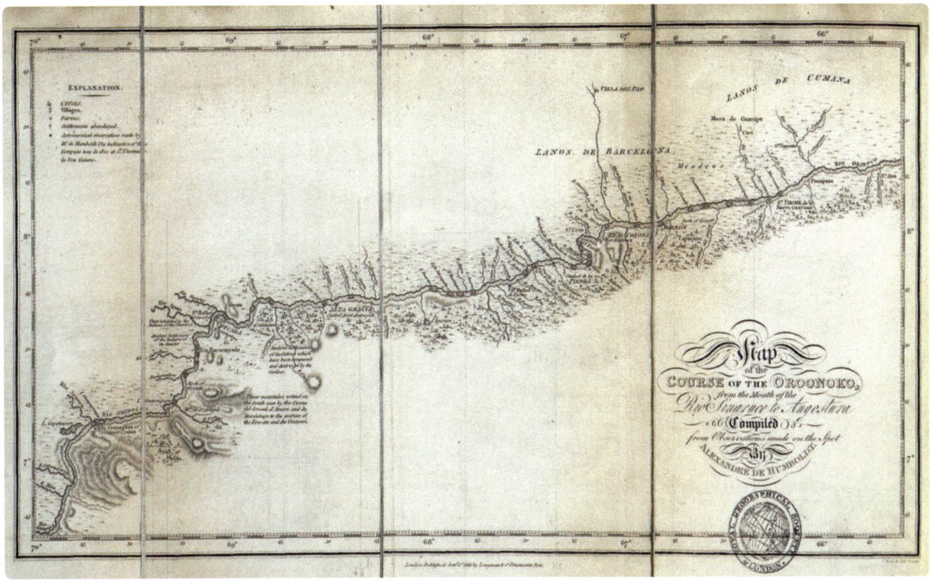

A detailed map of a section of the Orinoco River as pictured in Volume III of Humboldt's *Personal Narrative*. Naturalist Charles Darwin (1809–1882) claimed that "my whole course of life is due to having read and reread" Humboldt's book.

Travels with Bonpland

When his mother died in 1796, von Humboldt inherited a share of the family fortune. It was large enough to mean that he no longer needed to earn a living and could now indulge his passion for travel.

Together with his companion, the French botanist Aimé Bonpland (1773–1858), von Humboldt went first to Madrid, where the prime minister, Mariano de Urquijo, became their patron. With de Urquijo's support Humboldt and Bonpland decided to visit the Spanish colonies in South America, where they hoped to find out more about the geography, wildlife, and plants of the region.

Tracking the Great Rivers

There are two major river systems in northern South America, the Orinoco and the Amazon. Humboldt and Bonpland wanted to discover whether the systems were linked. The streams running into a main river in the area in which it rises are known as its headwaters; the two men set off for the headwaters of the Orinoco.

Their journey began with their crossing the treeless, grassy plains—known as the llanos—on foot, studying the plants and animals of the grasslands as they went.

They saw Amazon river dolphins (*Inia geoffrensis*) and entered waters that Humboldt was the first person to chart.

Near the town of San Carlos, close to the Brazilian frontier and beside the headwaters of the Orinoco, Humboldt and Bonpland found the Casiquiare canal, a natural waterway. Following this, they discovered that it led to the Negro River, which led in turn to the headwaters of the Amazon. This meant they had definitely established that the Orinoco River and the Amazon River were linked.

Crossing the Andes

After a stay in Cuba, the travelers returned to South America. Landing at Cartagena in

This 19th-century painting by Friedrich Georg Weitsch (1758–1828) imagines the scene as Humboldt and Bonpland arrive at the foot of the volcanic Mount Chimborazo. Chimborazo is the highest point in the Cordillera Real mountain range in Ecuador. Though the two men did not reach the summit, they still reached a higher altitude than anyone on record had ever done before.

Colombia in March 1801, they decided to travel through the mountains of the Andes to Lima. The entire region was then known as New Granada; it now makes up parts of Colombia, Ecuador, and Peru.

When they came to their first stop in Bogotá, now in Colombia, Bonpland fell ill, so they remained there until September and Humboldt continued working. Between them they had already found more than 3,000 previously undocumented new species of plants.

Mountains and Coasts

Arriving in Quito, they prepared to climb Mount Chimborazo, a volcano in Ecuador that is 20,548 feet (6,263 m) high. It was then thought to be the highest mountain in the world, but in fact Mount Everest in the Himalayas is much higher; Everest's peak stands at 29,028 feet (8,848 m). In June 1802, by now accomplished mountaineers, Humboldt and Bonpland climbed to about 18,893 feet (5,762 m) on Chimborazo, setting a world altitude record that was not broken until 36 years later, when Humboldt's friend the French chemist Joseph Gay-Lussac (1778–1850) ascended higher in a balloon.

Despite their climbing experience, Humboldt and Bonpland both suffered from mountain sickness, a complaint that Humboldt was the first person to recognize as being caused by a lack of oxygen in the high mountain air.

Studying Earth Sciences

Humboldt was a pioneer in the field we now know as Earth sciences; he believed that any study of Earth should involve all the different sciences concerned with the structure, age, and workings of Earth: physical geography, geology, meteorology, zoology, and botany. His aim was to construct a science that showed how everything was linked, so that he could understand "nature as a whole."

In Ecuador Humboldt had made a careful study of the many volcanoes of the area. He noticed that they invariably lie in straight lines. This, he established, was because they are found above faults (fractures) that lie deep in Earth's crust. He also observed that many of the rocks on Earth's surface are of igneous origin (igneous means "fiery"), showing that they were clearly formed in conditions of extreme heat.

The Magnetic Earth

Another area of study that fascinated Humboldt was Earth's magnetism. Today this falls within the academic field of geophysics, the study of the physical properties of the whole Earth, and in many ways Humboldt can be considered the inventor of this branch of science. Humboldt mapped Earth's magnetism over a substantial area during the course of his travels, discovering that its intensity was strongest at the north and south poles and weakest at the equator. Wherever he went he also measured the magnetic "dip" of a compass needle, which is the angle it makes with the horizontal as it points toward Earth. At 7°S he found the magnetic equator, the point at which his compass needle was horizontal. Humboldt also found that the compass needle sometimes swung rapidly

JOSEPH GAY-LUSSAC (1778-1850)

Joseph Gay-Lussac was born near Limoges in France in 1778, and attended the Polytechnic School in Paris before taking a post as assistant to the chemist Claude-Louis Berthollet. Gay-Lussac became interested in studying whether Earth's magnetic intensity changed with height; to investigate this he made trips in a hydrogen-filled balloon. It was on one such ascent that he beat Humboldt's altitude record. Experiments that he carried out with Humboldt established that one volume of oxygen combines with two volumes of hydrogen to form water; by 1808 Gay-Lussac had discovered that all gases combine in simple proportions by volume. In 1809 he became professor of physics at the Sorbonne and from 1832 was professor of chemistry in the botanic gardens in Paris, the Jardin des Plantes.

back and forth; he called these disturbances "magnetic storms." In fact it was not until the 20th century that scientists finally discovered these disturbances are caused by solar winds (electrically charged material thrown out by the sun), which disturb Earth's magnetic field.

Accounts of the Journey

Back in Paris after his travels, much of Humboldt's time was spent in writing up accounts of his journeys and discoveries. His *Essay on the Geography of Plants* (1805), which marked the beginning of the science of biogeography, made up Volume 5 of his major work, *Personal Narrative of Travels to the Equinoctial Regions of the New Continent.* He also wrote *A Political Essay on the Island of Cuba.* This was published in 1826, but not as part of the *Personal Narrative.*

By the time Humboldt had completed the Personal Narrative his inherited fortune was almost gone. When Frederick William III offered him the post of chamberlain—managing the king's household—Humboldt had little choice but to accept.

In 1827 Humboldt returned reluctantly to Berlin, where he stayed for the remaining 30 years of his life.

A painting of Alexander von Humboldt in his study in 1845. Between 1799 and 1804, he traveled around Latin America and wrote about his discoveries, which were published in an enormous set of volumes.

Last Work

For the last 20 years or so of his life Humboldt was engaged in writing *Cosmos*, a major work that he had been planning since about 1827. His aim was to present a description of Earth in which all the sciences were drawn together, as well as to counter the romantic, antiscientific philosophies that were becoming popular. It was the first comprehensive encyclopedia of geography and geology. *Cosmos* appeared in five volumes between 1845 and 1862, after Humboldt's death. Humboldt died aged 89 on May 6, 1859, and was given a state funeral.

SCIENTIFIC BACKGROUND

Before 1790

English physician William Gilbert (1540–1603) establishes that the Earth acts like a huge bar magnet

English botanist Joseph Banks (1744–1820) joins English navigator Captain James Cook (1728–1779) on his 1768–71 voyage around the world

German geologist Abraham Gottlob Werner (1749–1817) advocates his theory—known as Neptunism—that an ocean once covered the world

Scottish geologist James Hutton (1726–1797) suggests that the Earth is millions rather than thousands of years old

1790

1793 English chemist John Dalton (1766–1844) publishes *Meteorological Observations and Essays*. He has kept information about the weather since 1787 and will continue to do so until his death

1799 Von Humboldt and French botanist Aimé Bonpland (1773–1858) set out on a five-year trip to South America, Cuba, and Mexico

1800

1804 French chemist and physicist Joseph Gay-Lussac (1778–1850) ascends in a hot-air balloon to study the Earth's magnetism and the composition of the Earth's atmosphere

1805 Gay-Lussac and Humboldt present a statement to the French Academy of Sciences asserting that hydrogen and oxygen combine in a ratio of two to one to form water

1808 Gay-Lussac discovers that gases mix in simple proportions by volume

1810

1813 Swiss botanist Augustin Pyrame de Candolle (1778–1841) coins the word "taxonomy" to describe the classification of organisms

1815 English civil engineer William Smith (1769–1839), who has pioneered the study of fossils to identify the age of rock layers, publishes his *Geological Map of England and Wales and Part of Scotland*

1820

1824 Pyrame de Candolle begins his most famous work, *Treatise on the Natural System of the Plant Kingdom*

1825 German chemist Justus Liebig (1803–1873), who has studied under Gay-Lussac, becomes professor of chemistry at the university of Giessen

1828 Humboldt becomes a founder member of the Geographic Society

1830

1831 The British Association for the Advancement of Science is founded

1833 Swiss botanist Alphonse de Candolle (1806–1893), son of Augustin Pyrame de Candolle, publishes *The Origin of Cultivated Plants*

1834 Humboldt publishes the last volume of his *Personal Narrative*

1840 Swiss-born American naturalist Louis Agassiz (1807–1873) publishes *Studies on Glaciers*, further evidence to back his theory of an ice age, which has been ridiculed by Humboldt

1840

1843 The climatic importance of ocean currents is recognized by American hydrographer Matthew Fontaine Maury (1806–1873)

1845 The first volume of Humboldt's encyclopedia of geography and geology, *Cosmos*, is published; the last volume will be published in 1862, after his death

1848 The American Association for the Advancement of Science is founded

1850

1855 Alphonse de Candolle publishes *Rational Botanical Geography*

1860

After 1860

1862 Agassiz publishes the final part of his *Contributions to the Natural History of the United States*; it will be followed in 1867 with his account of *A Journey to Brazil*

1915 German meteorologist and geophysicist Alfred Wegener (1880–1930) puts forward his theory of continental drift — that the continents were once joined together but have slowly drifted apart. It is published in English in 1924 as *Origins of Continents and Oceans*

POLITICAL AND CULTURAL BACKGROUND

1789 In the United States the new constitution is adopted and George Washington (1732–1799) is named first chief-magistrate or president of the first U.S. government

1792 The English-born American revolutionary writer Thomas Paine (1737–1809) completes *The Rights of Man*, in which he supports the French Revolution and encourages the overthrow of the monarchy

1793 Louis XVI is tried and executed in Paris, one of more than 2,500 people to be guillotined in Paris during the Reign of Terror engineered by Maximilien Marie Isidore de Robespierre (1758–1794)

1801 Having been persuaded out of retirement, American politician Thomas Jefferson (1743–1826) is elected third president of the United States

1804 Napoleon Bonaparte (1769–1821) crowns himself emperor of France; meanwhile Austria, England, Russia, and Sweden mobilize forces to protect their lands against Napoleon's military ambitions

1807 A 19-year struggle by English philanthropist William Wilberforce (1759–1833) ends in success as the slave trade between Britain and its colonies is officially abolished; in the United States the trading of slaves with Africa is forbidden

1816 The American Colonization Society is founded to give freed slaves a new home; many African Americans migrate to a region in West Africa that in 1824 is named Liberia, from the Latin word *liber* meaning "free"

1818 English Romantic poets Percy Bysshe Shelley (1792–1822), John Keats (1705–1821), and Lord Byron (1788–1824) are at the height of their powers; *Ozymandias* by Shelley, *Endymion* by Keats, and the final canto of *Childe Harold's Pilgrimage* by Byron are all published this year

1820 American Primitive or folk artist Edward Hicks (1780–1849) begins his series *The Peaceable Kingdom*, based on the biblical verse from Isaiah 11:6, which predicts a time when "the wolf shall lie down with the lamb." Hicks will paint up to 100 variations on this theme

1830 In the United States the Indian Removal Act forces Native Americans to move west and surrender their own lands in exchange. The forcible eviction of the Cherokees in 1838–39, during which about 4,000 people die, becomes known as the "Trail of Tears"

1833 The American Anti-Slavery Society is founded by abolitionists including James Mott (d. 1868)

1840 Under the Treaty of Waitangi about 500 Maori chiefs surrender the sovereignty of New Zealand to Britain in return for guarantees on land and possessions. Breaches of the treaty lead the Maoris to embark on the first Maori War in 1843

1840 The first wave of mass immigration to the United States begins from Europe; more than 200,000 Irish people are among those making the journey

1846 US President James Polk (1795–1849) accuses Mexicans of spilling "American blood on American soil" as war breaks out between the two countries; in 1848 Mexico renounces claims to Texas and cedes New Mexico and California to the United States

1855 The first edition of *Leaves of Grass* by American Poet Walt Whitman (1819–1892) is published; subsequent editions expand the work with poems such as "Drum Taps," and "I Sing the Body Electric"

1861 In March Abraham Lincoln (1809–1865) is sworn in as the 16th president of the United States. South Carolina and the six Gulf states have seceded from the Union and formed the Confederate States of America, and civil war breaks out in June

Glossary

bathyscaphe A spherical submersible craft used for deep-sea exploration.

biodiversity The total diversity of organisms and genes in a given area.

biomass The total weight of all the organisms in an area (or trophic level).

biome A type of major ecological community, such as a tropical rain forest, desert, or tundra.

biosphere All the parts of Earth that are able to sustain life; includes the lower atmosphere, oceans, and the surface of the land and fresh waters, and extends to a mile or so below the surface.

brackish Semisalty water, as in estuaries and deltas.

canopy Uppermost level at the tops of trees in a forest.

carbon cycle The cycle of carbon through the natural world.

carnivore An animal that eats meat.

cellulose Tough chemical that forms part of the cell walls of plants.

CFC A chemical called a chlorofluorocarbon used in the manufacture of refrigerators, polystyrene, and in aerosol spray cans; it was a major depleter of the ozone layer.

climate The regular weather pattern that occurs in a certain region.

community A group of different species that share a habitat.

countershading Organisms with a light top surface and a darker lower surface are said to be countershaded; common in creatures that occur in surface waters, like penguins and plankton.

dark zone An area of the deep sea to which light from the surface cannot reach.

delta Land crossed by small water channels that forms around the mouth of a river through the laying down of sediment.

ecosystem An ecological unit that comprises a community of organisms and its environment.

euphotic zone The upper layer of the ocean that receives sunlight.

filter feeder An animal that sieves fine particles from water for food.

food chain The passage of energy between organisms; a plant links to a herbivore, which in turn links to a carnivore. Energy is lost with each step.

food web A complex series of interlinked food chains.

fossil fuel A carbon-based fuel, such as oil or coal, that forms from the remains of ancient organisms.

Gaia hypothesis The idea that Earth functions as an enormous "superorganism" that maintains the conditions necessary for its survival.

greenhouse effect The rise in global temperatures caused by an increase in gases such as methane and carbon dioxide in the atmosphere.

guano A phosphorus-rich fertilizer that consists of the droppings of seabirds.

habitat The type of place in which an organism lives.

herbicide A chemical that kills off pest plants such as weeds.

herbivore An animal that feeds on plants.

hibernation Spending the winter in an inactive or dormant state.

hydrothermal vent A crack in rocks deep under the sea from which streams of very hot, chemical-laden water well up from inside Earth's crust.

introduction The establishment of a species into a new area, sometimes through the activities of people.

mesosphere The atmospheric level between troposphere and stratosphere containing little water vapor, and where the temperature drops to -112°F (-80°C).

microhabitat A small part of a habitat that sustains a community; for example, a pool in the leaves of bromeliad plants forms a microhabitat.

migration The long-distance journey by animals such as birds, antelope, and whales either to escape harsh winter weather or to follow good sources of food.

monoculture The growing of just one crop over large areas of land.

natural selection The theory that only the organisms best suited to their environment survive to reproduce. Natural selection is the driving force behind evolution.

niche The ecological role of an organism in a community.

nitrogen fixation The incorporation by soil bacteria of nitrogen in the air into nitrate compounds that plants are able to use.

ozone layer The layer of ozone gas high in the atmosphere. It filters out harmful ultraviolet radiation from the sun.

pesticide A chemical that kills pest organisms.

photosynthesis The conversion of water and carbon dioxide into sugars in plants, using the energy of sunlight.

phytoplankton The plantlike algae that float in the surface waters of lakes or the ocean.

predator An animal that catches other animals for food.

prey An animal caught and eaten by another animal.

respiration The process of reacting food with oxygen to liberate energy; takes place inside the mitochondria of eukaryotes or on the cell membrane of prokaryotes like bacteria.

salinity The salt content of water.

savanna A tropical grassland.

stratosphere The second lowest level of the atmosphere. It contains the ozone layer and extends from the troposphere below to the mesosphere above.

territory An area controlled by an organism to protect food supplies or to attract a mate.

trophic level One of the links in a food chain; plants, herbivores, and carnivores are all at different trophic levels.

troposphere The lowest layer of the atmosphere. It contains most of the water vapor; clouds occur in this layer, and weather changes happen there.

tundra The cold, treeless near-polar region with a layer of permanently frozen soil just beneath the surface.

twilight zone The ocean level that receives only small amounts of light from the surface.

zooplankton Small animals that float in the surface waters of lakes or the ocean.

Further Information

American Association for the Advancement of Science
1200 New York Avenue NW
Washington, DC 20005
202-326-6400
Website: www.aaas.org
The AAAS is an international nonprofit organization dedicated to advancing science, engineering, and innovation around the world. It works to provide a voice for science topics, defend science and its use, promote the responsible use of science in public policy, and strengthen and diversify the science and technology workforce. It publishes the *Science* family of journals and is open to students.

American Museum of Natural History
200 Central Park West
New York, NY 10024-5102
(212) 769-5100
Website:www.amnh.org
This museum showcases hundreds of animal species and fossils from the history of life on Earth. The website offers information about visiting the site in New York City as well as online events and articles. The connected OLogy website focuses on science for kids.

The Nature Conservancy
4245 North Fairfax Drive, Suite 100
Arlington, VA 22203-1606
(703) 841-5300
Website: www.nature.org
This is the leading conservation organization working around the world to protect ecologically important lands and waters. The website provides online events, data and reports, and many ways to get involved.

New York Hall of Science
47-01 111th Street
Corona, NY 11368
718-699-1341
Website: www.nysci.org
Email: info@nysci.org
This hands-on science and technology center offers visitors the chance to participate in activities while learning about science. The website provides information about the physical site as well as details about many science activities to do at home.

The Science Museum
Exhibition Road
South Kensington
SW7 2DD
London UK
Website: www.sciencemuseum.org.uk
This science museum is renowned for its collections, galleries, and exhibitions dedicated to science. This site provides a way to explore and search the museum's collections online and learn about its many objects.

Wildlife Conservation Society
2300 Southern Boulevard
Bronx, NY 10460
(718) 220-5100
Website: www.wcs.org
Founded in 1895, the society is dedicated to protecting wildlife across the globe through education and action. The website offers news, information on reputable zoos and aquariums, details about the pandemic and climate crisis, and more.

Further Reading

Appello, Gaoa. *101 Ways to Help the Planet: A One Year Challenge*. L Dixon, 2020.

Berners-Lee, Mike. *There Is No Planet B: A Handbook for the Make or Break Years*. New York, NY: Cambridge University Press, 2021.

Cameron, Lily. *Simply Sustainable: Moving Toward Plastic-Free, Low-Waste Living*. Berkeley, CA: Ten Speed Press, 2021.

Fee, Natalie. *How to Save the World for Free*. London, UK: Laurence King Publishing, 2019.

Gale, Jen. *The Sustainable (ish) Living Guide*. Newnan, GA: Green Tree, 2020.

Hanson, Thor. *Hurricane Lizards and Plastic Squid: The Fraught and Fascinating Biology of Climate Change*. London, UK: Icon Books, 2021.

Heap, Tom. *39 Ways to Save the Planet*. London, UK: Ebury Press, 2021.

Igloo Books. *The (Nearly) Teenager's Guide to Changing the World*. London, UK: Bonnier Books, 2021.

Jameson, Connor Mark. *Silent Spring Revisited*. London, UK: A & C Black, 2019.

Juniper, Tony. *The Ecology Book: Big Ideas Simply Explained*. New York, NY: DK, 2019.

Latham, Donna. *Biomes: Discover the Earth's Ecosystems with Environmental Activities for Kids*. White River Junction, VT: Nomad Press, 2019.

Lonely Planet. *The Sustainable Travel Handbook*. Fort Mill, SC: 2020.

Morris, Jackie (Emma Thompson). *Letters to the Earth*. London, UK: William Collins, 2019.

Potenza, Alessandra. *You Can Save the Planet*. New York, NY: Scholastic, 2020.

Thunberg, Greta. *No One Is Too Small to Make a Difference*. New York, NY: Penguin, 2019.

Wilson-Powell. *Is It Really Green? Everyday Eco Dilemmas Answered*. New York, NY: DK, 2021.

Index

M

N

O

P

R

Photo Credits

Front Cover: Shutterstock: S. Blew.

Bridgeman Images: Royal Geographic Society, London, UK 81, **Getty Images:** Anchorage Daily News/McClatchy-Tribune 65, Apic/Hulton Archives 84, Auscape/UIG 73, Barrett & MacKay/All Canada Photos 45, De Agostini 78, 79, 82, 85, Henry Groskinsky/Time & Life Pictures 50b, Tom McHugh/Photo Researchers 60, Mint Images/Frans Lanting 74, Richard Olsenius/National Geographic Image Collection 71, Rischgitz/Hulton Archive 29, James L. Stanfield/National Geographic Image Collection 46, Mark Turner/Garden Picture Library 56, UIG 59, 77, 82; **iStock:** 27, Frank van den Bergh 55, Sergey Yeremin 68; **NOAA** 51; **Public Domain:** Charlottenjof Palace/Prussian Palaces and Gardens Foundation Berlin-Brandenburg 80; **Shutterstock:** 06photo 14, Agami Photo Agency 20, BearFotos 66, Sarah Barry 35, behindlens 52, 61, Volodymyr Burdiak 26, Rich Carey 50t, J Carr Photo 34, Chase Dekker 70, DanielXD 76, effective stock photos 54, David Evison 58, Evgeniy 6, Anna Flasker 30, FloridaStock 36, Elizaveta Galitckaia 22, Bryan Hall 44, harvepino 43, ID-VIDEO 17, Ken Kistler 72, lux300 63, MikhailP 28, Laverne Nash 75, Jens Otte 19, Real Window Creative 38, Dennis Silvas 41, sirtravelalot 69, Sundry Photography 11, Sunflowermomma 8, Sungham 67, testing 62, Vandathai 64, Various Images 40, WildlifeWorld 12; **Thinkstock:** Hemera 57.

All other photos and illustrations Brown Bear Books Ltd.